SPORTS IN AMERICA

edited by JANET PODELL

THE REFERENCE SHELF

Volume 57 Number 5

THE H. W. WILSON COMPANY

New York 1986

THE REFERENCE SHELF

The books in this series contain reprints of articles, excerpts from books, and addresses on current issues and social trends in the United States and other countries. There are six separately bound numbers in each volume, all of which are generally published in the same calendar year. One number is a collection of recent speeches; each of the others is devoted to a single subject and gives background information and discussion from various points of view, concluding with a comprehensive bibliography. Books in the series may be purchased individually or on subscription.

Library of Congress Cataloging in Publication Data

Main entry under title:

Sports in America.

(The Reference shelf ; v. 57, no. 5)
Bibliography: p.
1. Sports—United States—Addresses, essays,
lectures. I. Podell, Janet. II. Series.
GV583.S6858   1986   796'.0973   85-22656
ISBN 0-8242-0713-0

Printed in the United States of America

CONTENTS

PREFACE

Since World War II, American sport has become a mammoth industry that generates billions of dollars annually. Interest in sport is nearly universal. According to a recent survey, 96.3 percent of all Americans engage in some kind of regular sporting activity: 42 percent play sports themselves on a daily basis, but many more participate as spectators. Sportswatching is the "common denominator," the one collective activity that appeals to Americans of all races, ages, income levels, and educational backgrounds, and of both genders. Indeed, sportswatching may well be Americans' truest expression of democratic feeling: far more people watch sports than vote in national elections.

Clearly, sports give pleasure on a massive scale, but their ability to attract a large audience renders sports vulnerable to many kinds of exploitation, both legal and illegal. The illegal forms of exploitation include point-shaving schemes, doping of players, and payment of amateur athletes on college teams. The legal forms are more likely to be directed at the spectators: they range from advertisements—on everything from billboards to track shoes—to the sale of alcoholic beverages at stadiums. One might also include in this category the efforts of various groups to sell the public—especially children—an image of the athlete as hero. These efforts have met with a good deal of success; in some areas of the country sport is considered more important than academic subjects at the high school level, and many young people forgo an education in their obsession with participation in sports.

Organized sport has also been co-opted by government officials who use it to advance political goals that change from one administration to the next. When the United States was seeking better relations with the People's Republic of China in 1971, it sent over a table-tennis team, a gambit that was known as "ping-pong diplomacy." The communist and democratic countries have for years used sports events to further their rivalry, culminating in the Olympic boycotts of 1980 and 1984. And many sports events, the Olympics included, have become an excuse for displays of the cheapest and most aggressive kind of patriotic emotion, sometimes leading to outright violence.

Caught in the middle of these commercial and political power plays are the athletes. A minority of athletes attain fame and its rewards, in the form of enormous salaries and fees for product endorsements. Some of these superstars eventually enter show business or politics (for in American popular culture the worlds of sports, entertainment, and politics intersect). But, for the majority of athletes, the only substantial compensation is the gratification of effort and, perhaps, a brief appearance in the record books. Sometimes athletes pay for the privilege of competing with the loss of their health—in the case of boxers, for example, or athletes who have been forced to play while injured—or the loss of their future earning ability—as in the case of young football and basketball stars who play for college teams but never receive an education.

The essays and articles reprinted in this collection explore selected aspects of organized American sports. Section I focuses on the attempts of individual athletes to boost their performance with the aid of psychology, technology, nutrition, and—at the risk of their mental and physical health—illegal drugs and synthetic hormones. Section II widens the focus to examine sports as a major industry that systematically exploits the competitive ideal for profit, and also discusses some of the social costs of that exploitation. The connection between sports and violence, including the influence of aggressive displays on spectators, is the subject of Section III. The final section is devoted to the 1984 Summer Olympic Games, which were held in Los Angeles, California, and which gave the American press, public, and sports industry an opportunity to indulge the national passion for sports in full and obsessive force.

The editor wishes to thank the authors and publishers who have kindly granted permission to reprint the articles in this collection. Special thanks are due to Roger Podell for his assistance and his expertise in the field of sports.

JANET PODELL

September 1985

I. PERFORMANCE AND TECHNIQUE

EDITOR'S INTRODUCTION

The application of science and technology to athletic performance is having a major impact on American sports. Once, competitors depended mainly on their own strength and endurance and on the advice of coaches and trainers who were themselves former athletes. In the last two decades, however, a battery of new techniques, developed by a new breed of sports researchers, have made athletic ability increasingly subject to quantification and rationalization. Computer modeling, biomechanical analysis, instant videotape replay, and self-hypnosis help athletes gain insight into their movements and motivations and have contributed to many record-breaking efforts. Advances in sports medicine, a specialty that did not even exist a few years ago, enable injured athletes to return to competition more rapidly and with fewer problems. And athletes themselves increasingly look to sports technology to give them the "winning edge." Few serious competitors can afford to ignore any new technique that promises to improve their performance, especially if their opponents have adopted it; but such innovations, as Terry Todd points out in this section, have their Faustian side. Athletes who seek to gain aggressiveness and strength by ingesting steroids and other potent drugs, for example, risk psychological damage and early death.

Edwin Kiester Jr's article, reprinted from *Psychology Today,* focuses on the growing use of sports psychology in Olympic training. As Kiester points out, the benefits of psychological training undoubtedly exist, but elude easy explanation. James C. G. Conniff, in an article from *New York Times Magazine,* reviews the boom in sports medicine. Doctors and scientists have responded to the millions of sports-related injuries suffered by Americans every year with new medical treatments, new ways of analyzing motion and stress, and new research into the effects of nutrition, aging, and other factors on physical abilities. Other new ways to study athletic performance are offered by the emerging field of biomechanics, described in Dwight B. Davis' article from *High Technology*.

Anabolic steroids—hormone derivatives originally developed to treat certain kinds of illnesses—were introduced to athletes by doctors in the early 1950s. Since then, as former weightlifter Terry Todd explains in an article from *Sports Illustrated*, competitors in virtually every sport have turned to the use of steroids despite their well-documented adverse effects. "The hunger for an edge," writes Todd, "is an ancient one, intertwined with our need to excel."

THE PLAYING FIELDS OF THE MIND[1]

In the classic stance of the middle-distance runner, half-miler James Robinson of the University of California at Berkeley half-crouches at the starting line. Robinson feels good, primed for victory. His senses are so keenly tuned that he can actually hear his heartbeat, feel the grating of the cinders under his spikes.

When the gun sounds, he jumps off quickly, striding smoothly and easily in his marked lane. At the 100-meter "break," when the runners are allowed to leave the lanes they started in, he glides to the inside of the track and situates himself at his favorite position in the early going, fourth or fifth in the field.

Other runners surround him. Robinson is careful not to be bumped or boxed, but otherwise he ignores them, absorbed in the kinesthetic details of his own performance. For the first 400 meters, he maintains a steady pace and position, 10 or 15 meters off the lead, but matching strides with the front-runner.

At 600 meters, the leader increases the tempo. So does Robinson. Some of his rivals begin to fade, and he moves up to third place, then second. Robinson has a reputation as a fast finisher, and at 700 meters, he turns on the power. With each stride he

[1]Reprint of a magazine article by psychology writer Edwin Kiester Jr. *Psychology Today.* 18:18–25. Copyright © 1984 by the American Psychological Association. Reprinted by permission.

gains on the leader. The gap narrows to five meters, then four. With 50 meters to go, the two are elbow to elbow. The grandstand is on its feet, but Robinson is oblivious to the cheers as he gradually pulls away from the other runner and takes the undisputed lead.

A good three meters in front, he feels the tape break across his chest. He has won.

Five-foot-ten, 29-year-old James Robinson has run that race again and again, but usually in his head, not on a track. One of America's premier middle-distance runners . . . Robinson has learned to prepare himself for a race by mentally rehearsing every split second in advance, down to the hiss of his breath and the crunch under his feet. The imaginary victory is neither daydreaming nor vainglory. Robinson's mental rehearsal is aimed at providing that slight emotional lift that might mean the eyelash difference between first and second place in Olympic competition.

This Olympiad, top American athletes such as Robinson are being trained psychologically, as well as physically, for the Summer Games. Impressed with the widespread success of sports-psychology programs in the Soviet Union and East Germany, the United States Olympic Committee (U.S.O.C.) has inaugurated its own long-term drive for mental conditioning as a means of regaining American athletic superiority.

Governing bodies for seven major Olympic events—volleyball, fencing, cycling, archery, diving, weight lifting and track and field—have organized the Elite Athlete Project to concentrate on the leading male and female candidates for Olympic gold. The athletes, who usually train near their homes, are fed a steady stream of current research in athletics—not only in psychology but in biomechanics, exercise physiology, nutrition, podiatry and conditioning. They are brought together at regular intervals for intensive training sessions during which they also review these earlier lessons and view films of themselves and others to refine their techniques.

Olympic officials acknowledge that the effort is only in its infancy. "The Eastern-bloc countries are way ahead of us," says Kenneth S. Clarke, director of the U.S.O.C.'s Sports Medicine Division. "They have psychologists who travel with teams at the youth, adult and elite level. When it comes to delivering psychological services to the athletes, we can't touch them."

Still, in a field that has previously equated psychology with Knute Rockne's halftime pep talks to the Fighting Irish, any recognition of the importance of mental preparation is a giant step forward. "At this level of competition," says Michael Mahoney, a clinical psychologist who researches sports psychology at Pennsylvania State University, "the difference between two athletes is 20 percent physical and 80 percent mental."

Earlier this year, Robinson, along with four other half-milers and five of America's first-rank milers, gathered at an Elite Athlete Camp on the campus of Arizona State University in Phoenix. A staff of eight coaches, a nutritionist, podiatrist, chiropractor, psychologist and physiologist provided the expertise. The sessions were patterned after those previously held for rowers, divers, jumpers and weight throwers. There were group lectures all morning, after which each individual had a private consultation with each staff member.

Robert Nideffer of San Diego, a former diver and diving coach who helped pioneer the technique of attention-control training for athletes, was one of the volunteer sports psychologists at the camp. According to Nideffer, an athlete's problem, in any sport, is to maintain arousal—that peak at which all skills are sharpest—without slipping over the edge into loss of concentration or pressing too hard. Maintaining this optimum state is especially difficult for the athletes under Olympic pressure, Nideffer says.

"Minor irritations will become major," he told the athletes. "Multi-event athletes may have to wait two days between the first event and the second event. You may start your warm-up, and then you'll have to stop for an awards ceremony. You'll be distracted by the press. You'll want to please the home crowd."

A particular problem for American athletes, according to Nideffer, may be the fuss over steroids. Their use is banned by American authorities, but most Americans are convinced that Eastern Europeans employ these hormones to build body strength, because some steroids can't be detected in tests. "You're going to feel, 'How can I possibly win when they have an unfair advantage?' That negative thought alone can defeat you."

Distraction and overanxiety could produce many poor performances at Los Angeles, Nideffer says. He thinks such mental clutter increases the likelihood of false starts among keyed-up runners, more fouls by weight throwers and more injuries. In the hubbub, athletes may overlook important details they would ordinarily notice. In one international meet, according to Nideffer, a high jumper kept hitting the bar at a height he had previously cleared easily. After he had lost, the youth realized that the jumping pit was in a drainage area, and that his approach run was downhill.

"We know you can't control the unexpected," Niderffer says. "The secret is to prepare yourself in advance for these gaps and surprises. Learn to concentrate on the inner cues and to return to inward 'centering' at these points. Practice progressive relaxation and systematic mental rehearsal to train yourself to be sensitive to your feelings, so you can adjust them.

"One diver told us that he was anxious, breathing fast and shaky. He would hurry his dives and almost run to the end of the board. With relaxation, he has learned to turn his focus inward, breathe deeply and concentrate on feeling that breath so that it relaxes the lower body and lowers shoulder tension."

For runners, Nideffer points out that breaks in concentration may occur when another runner false-starts or if a runner is first up on the blocks and has to wait for the others. Runners may also lose their cool when someone overtakes them. In both cases, Nideffer says, the athlete should briefly redirect attention internally to restore equilibrium and then immediately redirect attention to external cues. He suggests that runners carry portable stereos to listen to relaxation tapes or music prior to the race, in order to provide distraction from negative thoughts.

"Mental preparation cannot be achieved the week before the Games," Nideffer says. "You must work on it in advance." He suggests that runners psych up for the Games in three ways:

Positive feedback: When Nideffer asked the group of top athletes at the camp, "How many of you have ever lacked confidence?" every hand went up. Several confessed that they frequently thought, "What am I doing here with people who can beat me?"

"Positive reinforcement doesn't make you run faster, but it does prevent you from slowing down," Nideffer says. He advocates that athletes surround themselves with reminders of success, such as victorious pictures of themselves, and recall their best races, "as a confidence pill."

Goal-setting: Nideffer tells runners to think less about the importance of victory, which could cause them to overstride or choke, and focus on meeting a certain inner goal. A 1,500-meter runner who lacks confidence might aim to run 3:39 rather than concentrating only on finishing first. Runners should avoid unreasonable expectations, which could cause them to tense up and actually perform below par. Rather than dwelling on the records of the competition, it's better for runners to think, "I'm going to run really well today."

Visualization and imagery: Nideffer advocates that runners imitate Robinson's imagery technique and train all their senses to imagine the race in advance. In addition to rehearsing the performance and mapping their strategy, athletes must be conscious of their feelings and emotions, so that they will be sensitive to any departure during the actual event. And they should conduct the rehearsal in "real time," just as though it were occurring. The technique of visual rehearsal was developed by Richard M. Suinn of Colorado State University. Suinn hooked an Alpine skier up to an electromyograph, which measures electrical activity of muscles, and had him imagine skiing down a run. He found that whenever the skier imagined himself hitting a jump or handling a difficult section of the course, the electromyograph would record a burst of activity.

Several athletes in addition to Robinson already follow parts of Nideffer's formula. Steve Ortiz, a miler and distance runner, mentally reruns his best races over and over during the week before a big meet. "By the time the race starts, I'm almost in a state of self-hypnosis," Ortiz says. "I'm really just floating along."

Many athletes use mental preparation and relaxation to overcome self-doubts. In one-on-one sessions at the camp, Roger Jones, a miler from Auburn, Alabama, acknowledged that he wasn't sure he deserved to be there. "I look around at other runners and think 'These guys can leave me in the dirt. What am I doing here?'"

Jones said that in one 1,500-meter race against Steve Scott, considered America's top miler, he was beaten almost before he started. "I was expecting a burner," he says. "Instead it was a slow pace. I thought, 'I should take the lead and pick it up.' But then I thought, 'You can't take the lead from Scott. You can't possibly beat him.' The time was 3:42, and yet I had run 3:39 in the heats, and I'm capable of running 3:35. I run my best when I'm the man to beat in a race. Then I'm totally different, fluid, smooth, like somebody pumped me up."

When Nideffer went over Jones's training schedule with him, he found that the runner divided his practice sessions into four segments, performing some at top pace, others at a slow pace. Nideffer told Jones to concentrate only on his attitude for one quarter. "Don't be concerned with details of performance or strategy, just your inner feelings. Concentrate on a single breath, how it feels as you draw it in, pull it into your lungs. Feel it deep in your abdomen. Feel what happens to the muscles in your chest and in your shoulders when you inhale. Feel what happens when you exhale.

"In your training log, record your negative thoughts: how frequent they are, when they occur, how long they persist. Make a list of things that build your confidence. Set goals independent of winning the race."

Personal problems can also affect performance, as in the case of one athlete who had moved away from home to concentrate on his training. His parents wanted him to be a champion but didn't want him to move. "They say, 'We need you here,'" he told Nideffer. "But this may be my only chance at the Olympics. If I remain at home, I can't train properly."

"A lot of athletes have personal problems that impair their performance," Nideffer says. "These are the same kinds of problems that happen to nonathletes, and about all we can do is provide support and empathy. If that's not enough, we can put them in touch with a psychologist near home."

In elite-athlete camps for other sports, similar lessons in mental preparation are taught, carefully fashioned to fit the requirement of the sport. Mental rehearsal is particularly important to divers, says Dennis Golden of Southern Illinois University at Carbondale, chairman of the sports-science committee for diving, who describes springboard competition at the world-class level as "almost 100 percent mental."

"Because timing is so critical in diving and gymnastics," Golden tells divers, "it is important to mentally experience the performance as you want it to be performed, including the sequence and the intensity."

World diving-champion Greg Louganis is a master at rehearsal, Golden says. He rehearses his dives from the perspective of an observer, watching someone else perform. He rehearses them from the diver's viewpoint, going over the kinesthetic cues as well as the visual ones. He rehearses them to music, coordinating timing with auditory recall.

Golden's divers are shown videotapes of diving champions and told to "feel" themselves going through the same motions. The tapes are shown again and again until the visualization becomes second nature.

In field events, in which an athlete must muster all his skills for one supreme individual effort, learning to "center" and reduce harmful tension is particularly important, according to Tom Petranoff, world-record holder in the javelin throw. Petranoff credits Nideffer's relaxation techniques for his 327-foot, 2-inch heave that established the mark. "On the day of that meet I focused on a spot on the runway for 10 to 20 seconds, just feeling my heartbeat and my shoulders lower, and then—boom—I took off."

For weight lifters, concentration is critical, according to psychologist Mahoney, himself a former weight lifter. "Can you imagine having all that weight over your head and losing your concentration?" This spring, Mahoney held a practice meet during which audiences yelled distracting remarks to teach lifters to control attention.

Both athletes and coaches seem to agree that Elite Training Camps are beneficial. Unfortunately, few, if any, of the five or six volunteer psychologists in the Elite Athlete Project will be on hand in Los Angeles. Under Olympic rules, each national team is assigned a quota for professional personnel, and all of those slots are expected to go to trainers and medical doctors. Possibly the psychologists will be on hand at the Olympic Village or in the grandstand, but they will not be permitted in the dressing rooms or on the field.

The real payoff for the project may not come this summer, however. U.S.O.C. officials acknowledge that they are pointing to 1988, and hope to establish a more structured program in psychological conditioning in the next four years. The initial steps have already been taken by the governing body of the American diving team, according to Golden.

Whether the benefits will actually be measurable in medals won cannot be predicted. Some say the outcome will be more subtle.

At the camp in Phoenix, a track coach told a story about the value of psychology in athletics. One day, the story goes, a sports reporter noticed a basketball coach giving white pills to his team before a game. He asked what the pills were.

"They're just sugar pills," the coach whispered.

"But what good do they do?" the reporter asked.

"None," the coach said. "But the players think they do, and they play better."

The reporter accosted one of the players and asked the same question. The player looked about nervously.

"They're just sugar," he said.

"Do they help you?"

"No," the player said. "But the coach thinks they do, so we take them."

MEDICINE CATCHES UP
WITH THE SPORTS BOOM[2]

Hippocrates and Galen—the precursors of today's physicians who specialize in sports medicine—are known to have been on hand when young men, naked and gleaming with the oil that kept

[2]Excerpted from an article by medical writer James C. G. Conniff. *New York Times Magazine.* 130:40+. O. 5, '80. Copyright © 1980 by The New York Times Company. Reprinted by permission.

the dust from their pores, pushed themselves to exhaustion in athletic endeavors at Olympia. Now, centuries later, as America enters its third decade of the Age of Exercise, more and more citizens, men and women of all ages, are subjecting themselves to the glories—and agonies—of some form of vigorous athletic activity. As a result, more and more physicians are being asked to stand by to treat the wounded, and the overall field of sports medicine is suddenly assuming a substantially greater role in the lives of contemporary Americans.

By current estimates, at least one of every three Americans over the age of 16 has been engaging during the last two decades in some form of aerobic (heart-pumping) activity on a regular basis—playing a rapid game of badminton, or volleyball, bicycling, jogging, swimming. Everyone agrees that this kind of activity has been generally healthful—but it also has its dark side. The number of injuries among all athletes has increased dramatically, and it is estimated that 17 million to 20 million injuries are now occurring among weekend athletes alone every year, costing them and their employers (in lost time) some $40 billion.

Thus, physicians and sports scientists are facing a wide range of difficult questions, such as: Can the adverse medical consequences of the fitness boom be reduced? Can people get into better shape without hurting themselves? Which people are suited for which sports? And should those who are injured throw in the towel and cease exercising?

. . . Accelerating advances have been made in recent years in research on the exercising body's cardiovascular, pulmonary, muscular, skeletal, metabolic, biomechanical and psychological characteristics. Some of the research has led to ingenious new methods of mending athletes' torn or injured bodies—including new ways to repair battered knees or ankles, lessen muscular pain and cope with exhaustion. The scientific work has also brought about the improvement of athletic performance through the development of sophisticated machinery that analyzes sports techniques—identifying strong points and flaws, for example—and the refinement of knowledge about how diet, hot weather or aging affects physical activity, and vice versa.

Despite these accomplishments, the expanding field of sports medicine is not in a state of total harmony. There is behind-the-scenes arguing over who is qualified to treat patients and over which methods of treatment are preferable or even valid. The contention exists in large part because sports medicine is currently in the process of virtually redefining itself. It is deciding what its future roles will be—whether, for instance, there should be greater emphasis on prevention, as opposed to the patch-and-repair philosophy that many believe has been characteristic of traditional American medicine.

The current crop of sports injuries goes beyond the routine pulled muscle and the torn ligament to a wide range of problems, from heart attacks to jogger's nipple (an irritation to the point of bleeding suffered by runners of both sexes who neglect to protect the upper body with an undershirt or proper running bra). But the field of sports medicine has become so many things to so many people in the treatment of these injuries that it is no longer an easy matter even to describe the discipline. One definition is provided by Dr. James A. Nicholas, the orthopedic surgeon who is team physician to the New York Jets, Cosmos and Knicks and founder-director of the Institute of Sports Medicine and Athletic Trauma at Manhattan's Lenox Hill Hospital. Dr. Nicholas has a formula that he calls the Seven P's. "The first P," he says, "is the Performer—the participant, and his or her physical and mental condition. The next consideration, and it's very important, is Performance—the demand that, say, tennis puts on the performer for strength in arms and legs, in endurance, or in some degree of flexibility and agility, coordination, balance and so on.

"The third P is Pathology," Dr. Nicholas says. "This is extremely important, because hardly anyone is free of pathology in the body to some degree from one's early life, whether it be inherited or acquired: poor vision, or flat feet, or a missing vertebra in the spine, or knock-knees, or bad backs, or loose kneecaps or joints, bursitis, tendinitis, broken bones early on, or torn ligaments of the knees.

"The fourth P is Prevention of injury, and you accomplish that in large part by making sure the fifth P—Prescription—provides people with the sports that are best for their particular builds. That, in turn, depends on the sixth P, the Practitioner—who does the prescribing, and who should be a qualified coach, doctor, trainer or parent. Finally, there is the seventh P—Practice—to develop the skill you must acquire, *without* hurting yourself."

Orthopedic surgeons in sports medicine like Dr. Nicholas conceive of the body in engineering terms, and this has made new methods of treatment possible. They view the body as a series of jointed sections, each successively dependent on the next—a vertical foot-bone-connected-to-the-ankle-bone column of linkages. Imbalance or distortion in a hip can cause problems somewhere else—say, in a knee or ankle—or a foot malfunction can throw a knee, hip or a spinal column out of line.

The result is impaired performance and pain—often in a body location distant from the real cause. Correspondingly, proper exercise, corrective surgery or a properly designed brace for one troublesome area may correct the others. The importance of orthopedic surgery in sports medicine has become so apparent and has such appeal to young doctors that last January, for example, more than 100 of them, 15 of whom were women, applied for just two residencies at Dr. Nicholas's Institute of Sports Medicine and Athletic Trauma—the first such hospital-based research facility in America.

One question that affects the sports-medicine research efforts now under way in more than a dozen other facilities throughout the country is the matter of what "normal" means in relation to fitness. In the opinion of many experts, there has been an underlying, peculiarly American and utterly false assumption affecting considerations of fitness. Sedentary habits that have become a way of life in our society have long been considered "normal"—witness such folklore pronunciamentos as that of Senator Chauncey M. Depew of New York, who is said to have maintained that he got his exercise by "acting as pallbearer to my friends who exercise," or the remark attributed to Robert M. Hutchins, while he was president of the University of Chicago, that whenever he felt like exercising he would lie down until the feeling went away. Since old Chauncey Depew did not lie down permanently until he was 94, in 1928, his version of inertial guidance appeared to carry a certain weight.

The sheer burden of evidence has forced sports-science researchers to formulate a new definition of what is normal. The
average American life style is not truly normal for the well-tuned
human body-machine—which, from the time when early man
ranged the continents, was designed to be *used* rather than merely
inhabited. The gospel according to sports science is that humans
need to keep the body-machine in trim to achieve a sense of physical and mental well-being—and that this can be done by putting
it in rhythmic motion as much as possible, in accordance with
one's individual capacity. It's quite normal, the experts insist, to
begin exercising regularly when you're still a child—and to realize that people over 40 are capable of attaining fitness goals that,
only a few years ago, might have been considered beyond their
reach.

Each year, as many as 10 million injuries of all kinds occur
among the 20 million to 25 million American children who are
involved in sports. Often, these injuries occur because youngsters
have been pressured to play contact sports by thoughtless parents,
or by coaches whose only goal is that of winning. Sports scientists
say that, too often, children are encouraged to play beyond their
capacity in games that are wrong for their body types. But, the
experts say, adequate "physical profiling" of these children would
have made it clear beforehand that they were engaging in sports
for which they were probably unsuited—as, for example, when
someone with a lean sprinter's physique is steered toward weight-
lifting or ice hockey, or when a heavy-boned youngster is pushed
toward competition in tennis or in the 100-yard dash instead of
in football or rugby.

Hidden pathology, too, can compound the basic error of
matching a particular physique with an unsuitable sport. Dr.
Gideon Ariel, who directs research facilities in both Amherst,
Mass., and Los Angeles, has spent most of the past decade developing a technique called "computerized biomechanical analysis,"
which is able to pick up more subtle elements of pathology than
the naked eye—or even the X-ray plate—can detect.

Dr. Ariel and his staff, studying athletes like marathoner Bill
Rodgers or members of the Dallas Cowboys football team, use
computerized instruments to measure a multitude of the forces

and motions that occur during athletic performance. The pressure of the feet of a running body, for example, is recorded on a piezo-electric force plate so sensitive it can adjust to the pressure that would be exerted by a fly alighting on it. Simultaneously, high-speed photography (at 200 to 300 frames per second) is used to record the sequential movements of the subject as he or she swings a discus. The values of these forces and motions for each athlete can be projected on the display console of a computer, appearing as a set of stick-type figures that show the action of the athlete. The "biomechanician" analyzes what he sees, and recommends changes in form and body posture that have enabled golfers to add 30 yards to a drive, place-kickers to improve yardage substantially and tennis players to exploit individual traits they didn't even know they had. Previously undiscovered pathology is often revealed, inferentially, in these analyses. Doctors can then suggest ways to compensate for the effects of old injuries or structural imbalances.

One surprising aspect of sports medicine is how its insights are of fascination to those who haven't the remotest interest in sports or fitness. For example, thanks to research physiologist David L. Costill, office workers all over America may be reassured about the usefulness of coffee. Dr. Costill, working at his Human Performance Laboratory at Ball State University in Indiana, has found that the caffeine in 2.5 cups of coffee, if taken one hour before exercising, can substantially improve endurance during moderately strenuous exertion. Dr. Costill says that blood and respiratory data indicate that caffeine increases the rate at which the exercising body draws on stored fat for energy and "spares the rate of glycogen depletion from skeletal muscle," thus extending the duration of the exercise beyond the point that, without the coffee, would have represented exhaustion.

The 1,700 members of the American Association of Fitness Directors in Business and Industry have been using the insights of sports medicine to get the employees of the association's 375 to 400 corporate members thinking about diet, smoking, stress, physical activity and health in general. The association's president, R. Keith Fogle, a Prudential Insurance executive, says his industry is actively involved because "we pay out all this money for sickness and death, so it just makes sense to try to turn things around by emphasizing health and fitness."

The number of runners and joggers in the United States has soared from an estimated 25 million in 1977 to 30 million today; every third pair of shoes sold in America is a pair of running shoes. A nationwide survey of 25 of the most popular sports projects an astonishing growth in the number of individuals who will be taking part in bicycling, ice skating, tennis, racquetball, skiing, swimming, water-skiing, wrestling, scuba diving—all activities in which broken bones, torn ligaments, heat stroke and even coronaries may occur.

Among adults, many of these injuries befall the members of a suddenly energized populace who take to field, track or deep water in disregard of their prior sedentary state. Dr. Kenneth H. Cooper, the author of "The New Aerobics" and founder of the Cooper Aerobics Center in Dallas, says he gives treadmill stress tests to would-be exercisers over the age of 35. The tests are cheap insurance to find out how well heart, lungs, blood vessels, joints and skeletal muscles are likely to take the strain before one embarks on any exercise program. With a passing grade, says Dr. Cooper, the candidate for fitness should expect to set aside three months for proper conditioning, starting with 15 minutes a day of aerobic exertion—enough to get the pulse rate up to 60 to 70 percent of maximum (220 minus your age)—on alternate days, and lengthening the time as the weeks pass.

Even after passing a stress test and achieving appropriate fitness goals, however, certain imperatives of training, competition and just plain vigorous exercising are in order. Here are a few of them:

• The first involves a comprehension of the role of lactic acid—the troubling byproduct of combustion in exercising muscles that brings on fatigue. Lactic acid is the byproduct of the partial burning of glycogen (the form in which carbohydrate as a fuel is stored in muscle tissue) in the exercising muscle. A crude analogy is the buildup of the deposits on automobile spark plugs and cylinder heads when hydrocarbons are only partially burned in an internal-combustion engine that is not quite tuned up for maximum performance. For anyone who is exercising, lactic acid tends to bog down the working muscle and cause fatigue. Exercise physiologists have found, however, that a light exercise such as walking—instead of resting after heavy exertion—will cut in half, from two hours to one, the amount of time it takes to complete the removal of lactic acid from the blood.

• During exercise, the body's difficulty in coping with an associated problem, heat dissipation, is compounded in hot weather. Sports scientists close ranks in recommending precautionary measures. They advise against waiting to feel thirsty before you drink, for example, because the body does not indicate its need for rehydration until it has lost two to four pounds of fluid. During exercise in hot weather—or during any extended exercise, even in cool weather—the formula for safeguarding against dehydration is to drink 8 to 12 ounces of fluid every 10 to 15 minutes.

• To adjust to performing efficiently in hot weather, the recommended formula is to begin with half of one's ordinary exercise load, and then to raise it 5 percent to 10 percent each day. Acclimatization will be nearly complete in about seven days.

• Cold drinks are not only permissible, they are best—because they are absorbed more quickly than liquids at body temperature. Even sucking ice won't bring on cramps, say the sports scientists—it will, in fact, get liquid more rapidly into the blood, and will also lower the temperature of the blood plasma. Commercial drinks and fruit juices, if consumed during exertion, should be diluted with half or even two-thirds the amount of water. This is because the sugar in them can cause cramps, and may even slow up the absorption of water.

• Porous white cotton clothing reflects the hot sun best while allowing for ventilation; it should be loose enough to permit sweating to cool the skin by evaporation.

• For victims of heat stroke, the proper procedure is to get the temperature down by using anything cold, including ice cubes. It is important to stop, however, once consciousness is regained and alertness returns, in order to avoid a too-sudden drop in body temperature that could also prove fatal.

• The sports scientists warn exercisers *never* to use salt tablets, because they can accelerate dehydration and lead to blood clots, kidney failure, heart attacks and strokes. The saltshaker should be used a *bit* more freely on foods, if one finds that a craving for salt develops.

It is in the realm of competition and efforts to affect the outcome that sports medicine has achieved its greatest notoriety. The more questionable techniques attributed to the discipline include the abuse of steroids to promote muscle development, the use of amphetamines and other drugs to heighten the competitive edge, and the use of "blood boosting" to enhance performance. Blood boosting is the practice of drawing off a portion of an athlete's blood and preserving it while the body replaces the "lost" red cells, and then reinfusing the preserved blood before an athletic competition. This, its practitioners maintain, increases blood volume, boosts the number of the athlete's red cells, saturates the blood with hemoglobin, increases the blood's oxygen-carrying capacity and thereby increases endurance.

But the picture of sports medicine as the instrument of athletic underhandedness is misleading. In Olympic competitions, all forms of "doping" are illegal, and officials have consistently resorted to sports science for help in policing the rules. For example, a computerized device, called a gas-chromatograph mass spectrometer, is used to analyze athletes' urine samples taken under supervision before each competitive event, so that technicians can scan for the presence of drugs. The instrument can detect as little as three parts per trillion of some 60 outlawed "controlled substances."

Furthermore, athletes have been making use of a number of new devices that are helping them in legitimate ways to improve their performance. One is known as a transcutaneous electrical nerve stimulator (its acronym is TENS—pronounced "tense," a word describing the opposite of the state that it induces). The TENS, when applied to the skin, creates tiny electrical impulses that are taken up by the underlying nerves to block signals from torn or overworked muscles—signals that the brain would otherwise interpret as pain. Dr. Irving I. Dardik, a vascular surgeon who is chairman of the United States Olympic Council on Sports Medicine, says he used the device with excellent results at Lake Placid on a speed skater who had a back problem, and treated an American hockey player's partially torn knee ligament. He uses the TENS because "it cuts down on the need for drugs significantly," he says. "You can actually suture patients while using this device, without having to give an injection."

Another device, made by an English bioelectronics firm, is a compact electrical pump that rhythmically forces air into hip boots, or knee-length boots, of synthetic material. This intermittent compression simulates a massage, preventing the pooling of blood in the extremities—blood laden with the lactic acid that contributes to fatigue after vigorous exercise. Dr. Dardik, as a vascular surgeon, finds that he is able to use the boots to fight weariness after being on his feet for hours in the operating room. As a runner, he adds, "I can put the boots on after a long run, plug in the pump, and after half an hour of having my venous blood pumped uphill, I feel the fatigue vanish to the point where I'm ready for another run." Hospitals are now using the pumps in a delicate process that aids patients afflicted with postsurgical swelling, as well as those with vein or lymph problems.

Orthopedists have also contributed a number of techniques to further the treatment of all patients, and not just athletes. For example, to ascertain the extent of damage in knee and ankle joints, surgeons can now insert a sterile, half-inch metal tube through a small incision directly into a joint. They employ an arthroscope (from the Greek for "joint-scanner") to look for torn ligaments or cartilage, calcium deposits, bone chips or spurs. Through the tube, a surgeon is able to introduce surgical instruments to repair the damage; as a result, many sidelined athletes are now being returned to action sooner than they used to be. The Japanese are using the slender tube to assess damage inside the spine. The late Dr. John Marshall, physician for the United States Olympic ski team, who died last winter in a plane crash on the way to Lake Placid, more clearly defined the anatomical landmarks inside the knee with regard to ligament structure, in ways that led many surgeons to modify their operations. "Marshall was the first young man of the group we have now who developed a strong feeling about sports medicine, and his anatomical studies were a great contribution," says Dr. Nicholas.

One of the most exciting spinoffs from sports medicine to emerge thus far is the employment of a process technically known as electromyographic biofeedback. It exploits the fact that muscle tissue continues to have electrical properties even when it is paralyzed. Investigators such as Dr. Steven L. Wolf at the Regional Rehabilitation Research and Training Center of Emory University in Atlanta have, since 1975, used the technique to restore limb movement and ambulation in hundreds of stroke victims ranging in age from 19 to the mid-80's. In some cases, Dr. Wolf says, the crippling effect of the stroke had been endured for as long as 20 years.

The effectiveness of electromyographic biofeedback depends upon the discovery that there is never complete immobility in the constituent musculature of a paralyzed limb. Instead, there is what Dr. Wolf calls "spasticity"—which means the stroke victims cannot move their muscles because the muscles are so very tight. Dr. Wolf and his associates place electrodes on the skin above "crippled" muscles to pick up their hidden electrical activity, and then amplify it so that patients can hear the sound on a beeping device, or see it displayed on a panel that lights up in progressive stages. Experiencing this vivid proof that their muscles are not "dead" helps the stroke patients, first, to relax the too-tight muscles, and then to increase the activity of muscles on the opposite side of the hand or arm or leg in a controlled manner. "I know that strokes are supposedly irreversible," says Dr. Wolf. "That's what everyone believes. Well, they're not, and we're proving it here and in 50 workshops a year that we give all around the United States."

Sports science is also focusing on how aging affects human performance, and vice versa. It has been something of an American cliché that, after age 50, it's all over, athletically. Fortunately, though, tough-minded citizens in their sixth, seventh and even eighth decades have been establishing new physical norms for the sports scientists to study.

In "Exercise Physiology: Nutrition, Energy and Human Performance," Dr. William D. McArdle and Drs. Frank and Victor Katch report a startling result of their work: that "at an extreme level of active living, for example, the maximum aerobic power ability of heart and lungs to process large volumes of blood and oxygen] of 50- and 60-year-olds in some cases exceeds that of 20-year-old college students."

In aging, it seems, body functions decline at different rates, which are often subject to modification by exercise. The Katches and Dr. McArdle, who is professor of physical education at New York's Queens College, tell about a remarkable case of muscular development in an older man whom they described as "perhaps the strongest man for his age in 1974." This individual had begun lifting weights at age 50. He became so good at it that in his 60's he could lift 405 pounds. Even at age 80, he was still able to press 398 pounds. For comparison, a 20-year-old untrained weight lifter can press 150 pounds.

Clarence DeMar, known as "Mr. Marathon," ran in the Boston Marathon into his 60's and, earlier, won several of them. Dr. Paul Milvy, a biophysicist with the Council on Environmental Quality in Washington, says there are lots of Americans in their 70's, 80's and even 90's out there running and otherwise keeping fit. He points to a number of recent studies which tend to support his belief that by doing so "they are retarding by as much as 50 percent the decline that aging causes across the whole range of physiologic function—heart action, wind, kidney detoxifying capacity, muscle mass." Dr. Milvy cites the case of a San Francisco hotel bellhop who kept on running very long distances after he was 100. "I believe he ran his last marathon at age 102," says Dr. Milvy.

Dr. Allan J. Ryan, who is among those active in sports-diet research, writes in the journal Science that, from about 400 B.C., "athletes in training have been nourished with diets rich in protein, especially meat. Since athletes of an earlier day subsisted on bread, cheese, fruit, fish and wine," there must have been some idea that eating the flesh of a superior animal would give a human being superior strength. He says, "Most coaches and athletes still place great reliance on high-protein intakes," despite the fact that "protein is not used as an energy source by the body except in starvation," or when the diet is grossly deficient in carbohydrates and fat.

Current studies of fat have led to the disquieting conclusion that Americans are second only to West Germans in the percentage of total caloric intake—that is, 40 to 50 percent of the average American diet is fat, against as high as 70 percent in some instances in West Germany. The World Health Organization prescribes for *athletes*—who burn up most of what they eat—not more than 27 to 33 percent fat, 13 to 15 percent protein, and 50 to 55 percent carbohydrates as the main source of energy. According to one recent estimate, Americans may continue to lug around more than half a million tons of excess fat, despite the exercise boom. Many of them still do not exercise enough. If they did, says Dr. McArdle, they could consume 5,000 calories a day of whatever they felt like eating, and do it without packing on any more fat than a marathon runner does at that calorie-intake level, or even 6,000 to 7,000 calories a day.

An average college-age man has 15 percent body fat; a woman the same age, 25 percent—for anatomic and reproductive reasons. Higher concentrations of hip fat in even the leanest women give them a floating advantage for the lower half of the body as swimmers. Male marathon runners have total body-fat values as low as 5 percent to 6 percent (females, 15 percent to 16 percent). Below these levels, males are dangerously close to their limit of 3 percent essential fat—that fat which is required for good health—and females to their low limit of 11 percent to 12 percent. Essential fat guards—and is a partial constituent of—the heart, spleen, kidneys, liver, brain, spinal cord and cell membranes.

According to Dr. McArdle, dieting alone, with no exercise, costs the body fat—but it also costs lean muscle tissue that no one can afford to lose. A judicious lowering of calorie intake, *plus exercise,* burns more fat and conserves the body's muscle mass. Some muscle tissue is lost in dieting, but dieting balanced with exercise would hold down that loss. Dr. McArdle says an easy way to lose weight—say 20 pounds—would be to blend exercise and diet this way: Set a goal of one pound a week, for a total diet-exercise program of 20 weeks. A pound of body fat is produced by 3,500 calories; so the daily deficit has to be 500 calories to take off one pound a week (seven times 500 equals 3,500). "But a half-hour of vigorous physical activity on three days a week—about 350 calories per workout—would cut the average required daily deficit from 500 to 350, or 1,050 calories weekly (three times 350 equals 1,050). Instead of having to cut food intake by 3,500 calories for that week, it would be necessary to cut back by only about 2,450. Increasing the number of exercise days to five a week would require a reduction in food intake by only 250 calories instead of 500. And increasing the time from 30 minutes to one hour, five days a week, would wipe out any remaining need to reduce the number of calories from food, because exercise alone would be burning up the 3,500 calories necessary to shed that pound of storage fat. In fact, if you increase the time and intensity of the exercise, you could actually eat more and still stay thin, as marathon runners do."

There is so much new information now available about exercise and the medical aspects of sports that the journal International Sports Sciences, published by the Franklin Institute Press in Philadelphia, prints abstracts of 350 to 400 new articles a month culled from 4,200 other professional journals. But just how fast does such information sift down to the grass-roots level of the general practitioner?

Not fast enough, says one physician, Dr. Joan Ullyot of San Francisco, the author of several iconoclastic books on sports medicine. One of her prime targets is medical education itself. "Traditional medical education in America does not prepare doctors to even *recognize* health when they see it," she says, "much less help people attain it. What compounds the problem is that people who do exercise have a lot of changes in their bodies which the disease-oriented physician can easily confuse with illness.

"One of our top male runners in California, a few years ago, happened to be in the Navy, and he volunteered for a special assignment that required him to undergo tests to make sure he was healthy enough because the assignment was hazardous. The doctors who gave him the tests were horrified to find all the results abnormal, including his electrocardiogram and blood tests. He had a pulse of about 38, which shocked them, and some enzymes elevated to a level you'd normally see only to signal an impending heart attack. They were so concerned they prescribed a complete three-week bed rest.

"What they didn't know, of course, was that he had been running 100 to 120 miles a week, training. When they put him on bed rest, needless to say, his E.K.G. reverted to what the doctors considered 'normal' and his pulse began to come up to 'normal' as he lay there *deconditioning*."

The California runner's enzymes came down too, Dr. Ullyot says, "thus throwing the best runner in northern California *back* into the doctors' idea of excellent physical condition. At the end of the three weeks, they said to him, 'We don't know what you had, but you're completely recovered.' It didn't make any difference that after the first two weeks the guy had phoned me—because he knew I was interested in athletes—to ask if I knew what was wrong with him. 'You don't have anything,' I told him. 'You're just a normal athlete.'

"Everything in American medicine is based on norms, but those norms are not derived from studying healthy people, but from considering as the 'norm' the basically sedentary, overweight society that has been ours for too many years. Part of these norms come from the insurance industry, and part from myths perpetuated by the textbooks in medicine.

"Medicine in America is disease-oriented. There's a lot of self-education going on now in the medical profession, especially among doctors who are interested in sports themselves, and that's where your new sports-medicine doctors are going to come from; but their formal training does not educate them for this role."

"Take Eric Heiden," says Dr. Ullyot of the five-time Olympic Gold Medal speed skater. "He wants to study sports medicine, but to do it he had to go to Norway," where sports medicine has been a recognized specialty for some time. The American Medical Association says because "the comprehensive practice of sports medicine cuts across almost all existing specialties," and because, in the "various fields of scientific research," there are "many practitioners who are nonphysicians," there is little likelihood "in the immediate future" that "there will be much interest from physicians to establish a specialty board in sports medicine." The problem, says the A.M.A., is that "medical schools have not incorporated teaching in sports medicine into their curricula, and there are no residency training programs in sports medicine" other than "a few short fellowships" for "physicians already qualified in orthopedic surgery."

Yet, the treatment of athletic injuries is already drawing upon the insights of many disciplines. While orthopedic surgeons fix broken bones and torn ligaments, psychiatrists focus on the mind-body link and its effect on performance. Nutritionists are suggesting diets that will best provide sufficient energy for athletic activity, and podiatrists measure patients for orthotic devices (the molded prostheses that are fitted to feet to correct physical imbalances), which can help clodhoppers to become joggers. And even though the A.M.A. has conducted a long war against chiropractors, last January—before the Olympic boycott—Dr. Dardik of the U.S. Olympic Council announced that accompanying the American staff would be Dr. George Goodheart, a Detroit chiropractor who did much of the basic work in the system of "applied kinesiology" that chiropractors use to treat injuries.

One of the umbrella organizations for those who study or practice sports science is the American College of Sports Medicine, which has more than 8,000 members. The group has a higher percentage of Ph.D.-equipped exercise physiologists than it has M.D.'s. In the words of a prominent orthopedic M.D., the "different levels of education" among American College members "make it difficult to work together in ways that everybody will understand." In fact, there are so many differing viewpoints in the field that Dr. Nicholas has called sports medicine "a jungle." Anyone who is concerned about the well-being of the ordinary athlete can only hope these viewpoints will ultimately converge so that fitness-seekers can get the same kind of care the world-class and professional athlete can now afford.

SPORTS BIOMECHANICS[3]

To eyes previously dazzled by state-of-the-art computer graphics and animation, it doesn't look like much. A lone stick figure strides silently across a display screen, with a peculiar gait that only a few would recognize as that of a competitive race walker. But the spindly character's rudimentary appearance belies its deeper significance: Over the past several years, this multitalented stick figure has become the symbol of sports biomechanics, an emerging movement in sports analysis and training. Though still in its formative stages, this field has already aided numerous athletes, many of whom will compete in this summer's Los Angeles Olympic Games.

In essence, biomechanics takes the principles of engineering and applies them to the human body. Within this realm the simple stick figure illustrates the essentials of an athlete's motion and technique. Created from high-speed films of performing athletes, the figure is just one aspect of sports biomechanics, which uses film, video, and electronic techniques to measure performance and suggest improvements.

Swimmers, for example, can use biomechanics to improve hand and arm leverage, kicking power, and body position to propel themselves with optimal efficiency. Biomechanics' sphere of influence extends even into team sports such as volleyball. Here the entire team is viewed as a single biomechanical system, and position analysis of the various players helps determine the best setup for certain game situations.

Initially, biomechanics research focused on medical applications such as linking improper walking techniques with physical maladies. But researchers have long recognized that biomechanics holds the potential to help the human machine perform athletics with more efficiency, speed, and power. Over the past decade, as equipment for data collection and analysis became more sophisti-

[3]Reprint of an article by Dwight B. Davis, a senior editor of *High Technology. High Technology.* 4:34–41. Reprinted with permission, *High Technology* magazine, July, 1984. Copyright © 1984 by High Technology Publishing Corporation, 38 Commercial Wharf, Boston, MA 02110.

cated, sports biomechanics began to blossom. This fruition has been aided by a growing academic respect for the field.

"Typically, sport was not considered an area of serious research, and most deans of engineering schools weren't particularly enthralled about their faculty studying it," says Charles Dillman, who taught biomechanics at the University of Illinois and at Pennsylvania State, and who now heads the U.S. Olympic Committee's biomechanics lab in Colorado Springs. During the 1970s, as interest in amateur and recreational sports grew, so did the impetus to apply engineering to athletic techniques and equipment, Dillman says.

Eventually a commercial market may develop for biomechanical analysis in the most popular participant sports, such as tennis and golf, and for professional sports such as football and baseball. But for now, activity is largely confined to research by specialists in Olympic sports.

Despite its newfound respectability, however, sports biomechanics has significant hurdles to overcome. Foremost is a lack of equipment designed specifically to aid biomechanical research. The field is simply not large enough to attract the attention of manufacturers, so most of the equipment has been jury-rigged for sports applications. On the human side, graduate schools have only recently begun to produce trained personnel. Biomechanics requires knowledge of such varied disciplines as physiology, engineering, computers, and mathematics, "and not everybody can be an expert in all those fields," says Dillman.

As for the benefits that athletes gain from biomechanical analysis and training, Dillman is cautious in his claims. "There are athletes who say that our biomechanical suggestions have helped them make improvements," he says, "and we wouldn't be doing this unless we felt we were making a contribution. But biomechanics is just part of the complete system. We now have sports physiology and biomechanics combined with good coaching, good facilities, dedicated athletes, and financial support. Without any one of those components, the system wouldn't operate."

Olympic lab. The USOC's biomechanics lab was established in the late '70s under the guidance of Gideon Ariel. Recognized as one of the pioneers in sports biomechanics, Ariel now serves as president of the Coto Research Center (Trabuco Canyon, Cal.), a commercial biomechanics laboratory.

The Olympic lab—part of the USOC's sports medicine program, along with sports physiology, clinical services, and education—is considered by most experts to be one of the best-equipped biomechanics facilities in the world. Most of the equipment is state-of-the-art and is donated by manufacturers, often in exchange for feedback from the lab about equipment design and application.

Although Dillman believes the U.S. is second to none in its equipment technology—makeshift though it may be—he says the Soviet Union probably has the best group of sports scientists in the world. "But the Soviet researchers aren't too good at communicating with the coaches," he says, adding that in terms of implementing biomechanics research, no one yet matches the East Germans. But Dillman maintains that the U.S. has "the potential to combine both of these elements and become the best in the world."

Aside from conducting its own research, the USOC lab commissions and coordinates research at various other biomechanics facilities, mostly at universities, throughout the country. This way the Olympic Committee is able to tap the expertise of researchers who specialize in different sports. Only five or six of the more than 30 Olympic sports (winter and summer) are studied primarily by the Colorado Springs lab. Within these sports, the lab focuses its attention on a selected number of "elite" athletes thought to be likely competitors in the Olympic Games.

Requests for specific types of biomechanics research are submitted to the USOC lab by the national governing bodies of the various sports. When results are obtained, the lab makes them available to the appropriate governing body, which then disseminates the information to the coaches and athletes. The critical role, according to Dillman, is played by coaches.

"It's a typical misconception that scientists are working directly with the athletes," he says. "That's not true. None of our recommendations, no matter how good, can be implemented instantaneously. So the coach is still the central figure in the system for improving athletic performance, because it's the art of implementing the scientific information that is really the key."

Equipment galore. To give coaches useful information, biomechanists use an array of equipment to collect performance data. This equipment can be grouped into two major categories: electronic and film/video. Electronic equipment directly measures movement and forces. But because the athlete must either wear or come into direct contact with elements of such systems, they are most often used only in the laboratory. To collect biomechanical data from actual competition, researchers must rely upon unobtrusive high-speed film or video. Data analysis is carried out with the aid of computers, which typically run custom-written software.

Probably the most established piece of electronic equipment is the force plate. Depending on the sport, an athlete stands on, walks over, or runs across a plate embedded in the laboratory floor or racing track. For both static (standing) and dynamic (moving) tests, the plate measures various force components produced by the athlete. The USOC lab uses plates manufactured by Kistler Instrument Corp. (Amherst, N.Y.) and by Advanced Mechanical Technology (Newton, Mass.).

To measure forces, the plates exploit the piezoelectric effect, which causes an electrical charge to appear on the surface of certain crystals when they are mechanically stressed. For example, quartz sheets can be cut so they are sensitive only to downward pressure or to shear in a single direction. Layers of such sheets can be arranged in force plates in such a way as to be sensitive to downward, forward-and-backward (medial), and side-to-side (lateral) forces. Movement about a vertical axis can also be determined. Electrical charges produced by these force transducers are converted into voltages, which can be recorded and plotted. Kistler claims its force plate is sensitive enough to detect the heartbeat of a person standing on it.

In a static application of this technology the USOC lab measures the movement of archers and marksmen who shoot while standing on the force plates. "We're very interested in studying the movement patterns just before the shot," explains Janet

Dufek, a research technician. "For this application, the forward-backward and side-to-side forces are more important than the vertical force."

"For shooting and archery," says Dufek, "we're finding that it's not good practice to compare athletes or to model them after a world champion." For example, graphs of two archers show them leaning in the opposite direction from each other with one exhibiting greater overall stability. But in the two shots graphed, the scores were the same: 9 out of a possible 10. "Regardless of what movement or lack of movement occurs, " concludes Dufek, it's best to aim for "consistency within the subject from shot to shot."

But in other sports, such as running and jumping, the goal tends more toward emulating the technique of top performers. Biomechanics must work in concert with physiological capabilities and mental attitude in athletic competition; hence it's conceivable that a world champion might have a less than perfect biomechanical technique. But Dillman says that, as a rule, top athletes vary only slightly in their methods and that biomechanics theory tends to suggest techniques that these athletes are already using. "The top athletes do things in common that you can logically back up by applying principles of mechanics," he says. "So modeling after what the best in the world are doing has some justification."

Portable sensor. Force platforms are an important source of data for dynamic sports as well as static. A runner's or race walker's foot striking the platform provides information about the development and amount of force generated along the foot and about potential problems such as excessive sideward rolling (pronation) of the ankle joint. But there are limits to the practicality of force plates in dynamic applications.

A force plate large enough to measure just a single foot strike can cost $50,000. Long force platforms or series of small ones that can measure complete strides are often prohibitively expensive. Thus a complete evaluation may require that an athlete make several passes over a small pad, accurately striking it a number of times with first the right and then the left foot. The separate data are then compiled to yield a representative full stride.

A relatively new device from Langer Biomechanics (Deer Park, N.Y.) attempts to remedy some of the force plate's shortcomings. The Langer Electrodynogram (EDG) consists of 14 transducers that adhere to the soles of the feet (seven per foot), lead wires, and a data collection pack that is worn around the waist. Developed for podiatric gait and ambulation studies, the EDG has been a boon to the USOC lab, especially in the analysis of race walking.

The EDG is worn by an athlete either in a laboratory or in the field. To initiate a test, the athlete pushes a button on the data pack (or the test may be initiated remotely via telemetry). After a one-second delay, the EDG collects data for five seconds. This is long enough to measure several successive strides of a race walker.

Unlike the force platform, the EDG measures just one force component: direct pressure. And while force platforms detect the forces generated where the shoe meets the surface, the EDG measures foot forces within the shoe. These measurements tend to be more useful than the force platform data, asserts Michael Polchaninoff, Langer's VP of technical R&D and the developer of the EDG.

The EDG foot sensors are placed under seven bony prominences that biomechanical analysis has shown to be key areas of force transfer. "The detail available from the EDG, because of its isolated locations, is specific to the function and the anatomy of the foot," says Polchaninoff. He points out that two athletes with very different feet could produce similar force plate measurements once their bodies' force had been transferred through shoes containing corrective orthotics. "On the other hand, there are applications where you need to know about things like shear, which we cannot measure directly," he admits.

Even though it measures only direct pressure, however, the EDG can indicate motion such as pronation. The shifting of force from sensors on one side of the foot to those on the other side gives information about foot rolling, for example. And sensors placed in nonstandard locations like the side of the foot can measure lateral forces.

Each EDG sensor consists of a disposable adhesive component and a permanent component attached to the wire leads that link to the waist-mounted force-data collector. Together the two sensor components form a transducer system based on resistive principles. A force imparted to each sensor produces a corresponding electrical resistance, which is measured by the waist recorder. The information can be unloaded onto a cassette tape, permitting numerous field tests, or can be fed directly into a microcomputer dedicated to analyzing the data. Langer has a database of parameters for normal nonathletic walking. But because race walking and running results vary considerably from this standard, the company is relying on the Colorado Springs lab to generate databases for athletic application.

At some point the fairly bulky EDG waist pack may be eliminated and replaced with a telemetry system that would broadcast continuously to a nearby data collector. The USOC lab is experimenting with various telemetry applications in other fields, but director Dillman says the technology is far from perfected. And Polchaninoff notes that while it is possible to switch the waist pack on via telemetry, "it is difficult to transmit data at the rate and reliability we need over 14 channels."

Optoelectronics. Sports biomechanists care not only about the body's exerted forces but also about its movement. One piece of equipment—the Selspot, from Selcom (Valdese, N.C.)—consists of one or more cameras sensitive to infrared light. The cameras detect infrared waves produced by a variable number of light-emitting diodes (LEDs) that are attached to specific points on an athlete's body. The LEDs are turned on and off successively by an "administration unit," which also coordinates the camera sampling and transmits data to a computer for analysis. The cameras track the position of each LED as it moves across the field of view, producing data that can be used to automatically generate stick figures on a computer screen and parameters such as position, velocity, acceleration, center of mass, and body angles.

The latest version of the Selspot can support up to 16 cameras and 120 LEDs. With one camera and one LED, the system produces 10,000 samples per second. If 10 LEDs are used, flashing sequentially, the sample rate for each is 1000 per second. A single camera gives two-dimensional data on the athlete's movement; two or more cameras positioned properly can give three-dimensional data.

The USOC lab uses the Selspot system to measure apparatus movement as well as body movement, says Dufek. "We can apply the diodes to various points on the athletes or on the instruments they use, such as a marksman's gun, an archer's bow, or a weight lifter's bar. It gives us immediate feedback on those points in space, which we can then calibrate and analyze." Like the other electronic systems, however, the Selspot would be impractical in actual competition.

Film digitization. Traditionally, biomechanists have depended on high-speed film to capture detailed images of athletes in competition. For most sports, 100-frame-per-second film suffices, says USOC researcher Dufek, although sports such as golf, tennis, and baseball may require higher-speed film.

The USOC affiliate laboratory at the University of Kentucky, in Lexington, uses high-speed film to record and analyze the performance of sprinters and hurdlers in competition. The Kentucky researchers typically employ three cameras—one for panning and two for focusing on a specific area from different angles. By an algorithm called direct linear transformation (DLT), it's possible to get three-dimensional data from two fixed cameras. But although the Kentucky lab is equipped to calculate DLT, the track events being studied don't lend themselves to such analysis, says associate professor Ralph Mann, a chief biomechanics investigator.

The DLT algorithm permits only limited flexibility in camera angles and distances—parameters that are difficult to meet in setting up the equipment at a track meet, Mann explains. Some relatively confined events such as the high-jump and the hammer throw can be more easily filmed for DLT analysis, he says, "but the usual problem for us is that we have eight athletes competing in eight different lanes. Because of the situation's complexity, we can only perform a two-camera, two-dimensional analysis."

While a frame-by-frame observation of the film can yield qualitative biomechanical information to the trained eye, the images must be digitized and stored in a computer to produce quantitative data.

To determine the coordinates of an athlete's body as it performs, the high-speed film is projected frame by frame onto a large digitizing table. The USOC lab uses a table from Talos Systems (Scottsdale, Ariz.) with a resolution of 1000 lines per inch. The researcher uses a cursor instrument to enter specific coordinates from the image, such as toe, heel, knee, hip, and shoulder points. As the points are entered, a corresponding stick figure appears on a Megatek (San Diego) graphics display. At this stage, the figure gives a visual confirmation that the data have been entered in the proper order, ensuring their reliability. This process is then repeated, frame by frame. Although the manual entering of body coordinate data is tedious, no automated method exists. (The Selspot LED system can automatically generate stick figures, but it can't be used in competition.)

Stick-figure generation and the underlying data analysis are performed with software written by the lab's programmers and run on a donated Eclipse S/250 computer, made by Data General in Westboro, Mass. (The programs originally developed by Gideon Ariel are no longer used at the USOC lab because equipment modification has made them incompatible with the current setup.) The lab is also testing parts of a commercial software package developed by Herbert Hatze, a mathematician who directs the Austrian Institute of Sport in Vienna. Hatze's $30,000 Biomliv package covers functions ranging from basic kinematics to computer simulation "and represents the state of the art in mathematical analysis of the human body," says Dillman.

One of the USOC lab's main goals is to interface its own computer programs to the Hatze software, says Mark Fenton, a research assistant at the lab. But even with the lab's present custom software, biomechanists can move the stick figure automatically or manually, view every frame or selected frames, calculate the center of gravity and superimpose it as a dot on the figure, and determine the angles of the body segments. They can also set bounds for certain parameters, such as the angle of the elbow. If, for example, the angle exceeds 90° at any point, the system can be programmed to highlight the bending arm in a different color.

"We can also look at stride rate and stride length and compare them among different athletes, normalizing by body height," says Fenton. "One guy might make a stride that's 80% of his height, and another might make one that's 95% of his height. To determine which is better, you might compare them with the current world champion."

Fenton, himself an elite-class race walker, believes such biomechanical analysis has helped him improve his technique. Force platform analysis indicated that he decelerated at a certain point in his striding cycle. Analysis of his digitized film image showed that this deceleration was probably caused by a tendency to place his leading foot too far in front of his center of gravity. "I would shift back as I got the foot out in front of me, then pull over and shift forward," he says. "The shift back in the early support phase was probably an inefficiency, causing deceleration."

A race walker's legs should mimic the spokes of a wheel, Fenton explains. They should pass under the center of gravity, impart their downward and backward forces, and propel the walker smoothly forward. By shortening his stride slightly and making other adjustments, Fenton hopes to bring his technique closer to this ideal.

Video momentum. Although high-speed film has long reigned as the premier method of collecting movement data, its dominance may soon be threatened by high-speed video. Video has several advantages over film: It is inexpensive and easy to replicate, gives instant feedback, and records in dim light. Furthermore, two video cameras can record simultaneously on a single videotape for split-screen display of an athlete from different angles. And more people have access to video cassette recorders than to 8- or 16-mm film projectors.

Still, video has one major fault. "Its resolution is horrendous," says Mann at the University of Kentucky. A standard video signal produces about 200 horizontal lines across a TV screen. By comparison, film might have a resolution of 10,000 lines across the same area, Mann says, depending on the resolution of the digitizing table.

The resolution problem of video is related to the field of view, Mann explains. "If you attempt to analyze someone sprinting across a 10-square-foot field of view, any part of the body would have to move about two inches before you got a discrete point difference. That's unacceptable." Mann notes that if the field is limited to one or two square feet, the resolution is a reasonable quarter-inch or so. But such limited fields are feasible only for such applications as focusing on an archer's bow or recording a runner's feet on a treadmill. "For analysis of most competition, we will have to continue to use film for some time," he predicts.

Despite its current problems, however, video holds great potential, according to the Olympic lab researchers. Along with its low cost and ease of use, for example, video allows researchers to imprint simultaneous timing or force data on the videotape. An even greater benefit is that video output can be fed directly to computers for display and analysis.

The USOC lab is experimenting with a component board from Tecmar (Solon, Ohio) that digitizes a video input to an IBM personal computer. The digitized frame can then be displayed on a color monitor. Future developments in pattern recognition and other image analysis techniques might one day permit the automatic location and tracking of body parts in the digitized video frames, says Leonard Jansen, the lab's staff programmer. But for now, the goal is to be able to use an on-screen cursor to manually input the same body-coordinate data now obtained from film projected onto a digitizing table. The screen's cursor could be moved by a mouse pointing device or by a small digitizing tablet and pen.

One drawback of digitized video is that everything in the frame—even extraneous detail—is digitized, resulting in large storage requirements. But this could be overcome by equipment that permits digitization of nothing but the athlete's outline.

Regardless of the equipment used, a growing trend is the integration of data recorded simultaneously by different types of devices. For example, an archer might perform on a force plate while Selspot LEDs record the bow's movement. Depending on the equipment, the recordings can be synchronized by electrical or light pulses or, for events such as shooting, by an audio signal.

Central database. Such integration will enable the combination of biomechanical and physiological information. The Olympic biomechanics lab currently performs only a few studies jointly with its sister physiology lab. But an imminent upgrading of the USOC computer facility will help link the two labs more closely.

Data General will soon replace the biomechanics lab's Eclipse S/250 minicomputer with a 32-bit MV-series superminicomputer. The firm is also donating several of its powerful Desktop microcomputers. Dillman, who heads the computer facility as well as the biomechanics lab, says the MV will permit the sports medicine labs to process most of their work on a single machine.

Rather than use one type of microcomputer to analyze the Langer EDG results, another to digitize video, and so on, the new arrangement will facilitate the interchange of data among programs, including those that contain physiological information. The minicomputer will also serve as a central database of information provided by, and available to, biomechanics labs around the country.

The new computer will give electronic access to kinds of information already freely disseminated in print. Biomechanics results collected by the USOC and affiliated labs are published in reports available to anyone, including other nations. "From the Olympic Committee's point of view, there's no secrecy in this material," says Dillman. "There are six or seven countries in the world that can produce the same kind of information as we can. The real key is the implementation, not the uniqueness, of the results."

Only two types of information are restricted: the names of the athletes and particulars on equipment design (for instance, biomechanics data being used to design a new racing bicycle at California State University, Long Beach). So far, however, the USOC lab has done little work in equipment analysis and design. "Ninety percent of the requests from the national governing bodies are related to technique and performance," Dillman explains. "Consequently, that's where most of our effort is right now."

Future dilemmas. As currently practiced, sports biomechanics is unintrusive and relatively free of criticism. Using technology to analyze an athlete's performance and then working with a coach to devise training methods is far different from using steroids or other drugs to enhance performance. But biomechanics could eventually stray into controversial areas, and Dillman says sports associations will soon have to make rulings on just how far researchers can go.

"We already have the technology to put transducers into muscles and fire them from a remote site to increase the force of the muscle contraction," he says. "We could do that tomorrow. But our philosophy is that we're just trying to reach a point where we can help each athlete reach his or her own natural potential. Obviously, you can go beyond that and get into manipulation. Then Olympic competition could become a competition among scientists, not athletes. It's a problem the sports world will have to deal with."

For now, sports biomechanics depends as much on astute coaching and hard work by the athlete as on computer analysis and electronic gadgetry. And its impact is rarely immediate or stunning. "It's not something where you say, 'Hey, hold your arm a bit differently,' and the next day he holds his arm a bit differently and—bang!—there's a dramatic improvement," says walker/researcher Fenton. "So often with biomechanics, improvements come from working with an athlete over a long period." Nevertheless, he notes, a seemingly trivial change in a runner's or race walker's stride can add up over the many strides taken during a race: "It can make the difference between winning and losing."

THE STEROID PREDICAMENT[4]

What follows are my best recollections of how I felt about anabolic steroids as an aspiring athlete, what I have learned about steroids in the past 20 years and how my feelings have changed over that time. I make no claim of objectivity, having had a front-row

[4]Reprint of a magazine article by journalist and former competitive weightlifter Terry Todd. *Sports Illustrated.* 59:62–63+. Ag. 1, '83. Copyright © 1983 Dr. Terry Todd, University of Texas, Austin. All rights reserved. Reprinted by permission.

seat. I've watched what was at first a "secret" drug known only to a handful of elite weightlifters become a phenomenon so widespread that a majority of recent Olympic athletes, male and female, in track and field and the strength sports, are believed to have used some form of steroid; a phenomenon so widespread that pro football players have told me that as many as 50% of the active NFL linemen and linebackers have used steroids with the intent of improving their performance; a phenomenon so widespread that reports surface from time to time of teen-agers being advised by their high school, or even junior high school, coaches to take steroids.

The term anabolic steroid refers to various synthetic derivatives of the male hormone testosterone that have been developed through the years by the pharmaceutical industry to stimulate a building-up, or anabolic, process in the body. This involves the synthesis of protein for muscle growth and tissue repair. Normally, one way the body is helped in meeting its anabolic requirements is through the effects of the naturally occurring testosterone, which is produced primarily in the testes. Testosterone has both anabolic effects and masculinizing, or androgenic, effects. The androgenic effects—aggressiveness, facial hair, deepened voice, body fat reduction, increased libido, etc.—were significantly reduced several decades ago by biochemists who manipulated the molecular structure of testosterone to increase certain of its properties and decrease others. There was a medical need in the treatment of debilitating illness or severe accidents, which involve the breakdown of body protein, for a substance with a high anabolic–low androgenic effect, and Ciba Pharmaceutical Company responded in the late 1950s with an anabolic steroid called methandrostenolone. Trade name: Dianabol.

I first heard of Dianabol in 1962 from some weightlifter friends who had gone from Austin, Texas to York, Pa. to learn from the lifting champions of the York Barbell Club the best way to use the newest rage in strength-building techniques, isometric contraction, which consisted of straining against an immovable object.

What had been puzzling my training partners and me was that we'd been unable to make much progress at home, though isometric contraction was being heavily publicized as a real strength training breakthrough by the York Barbell Company's magazine, *Strength and Health*. It wasn't that any of us lacked the capacity for hard work or faith in the new system. Our faith arose from our observation over the previous year or so of the startling advances in power and musculature made by a veteran lifter from our area who, after years of having been good, but hardly great, had switched to isometric contraction.

The lifter was in his mid-30s, and it was an especially bitter blow to our young manhood—most of us were in our early 20s at the time—to have his progress so far outstrip our own. Isometric contraction was reminiscent of the old Charles Atlas system of Dynamic Tension, but however much fun we had yukking it up about 97-pound weaklings having sand kicked in their faces, we were willing to try any program that could apparently produce the gains in size and strength that we coveted. We thought we understood the new system, but though we huffed and puffed and even ruptured an occasional capillary, we failed to make much progress. Meanwhile, our 35-year-old friend continued making remarkable advances.

Bob Hoffman, the York Barbell Company's president, had published an article on isometric contraction in November 1961. He subtitled it "The Most Important Article I Ever Wrote," and it began, "I am about to tell you about the greatest system of physical training, the greatest system of strength and muscle building the world has ever seen."

The article continued in that vein and outlined the theoretical principles, originally formulated by Theodor Hettinger and Erich Müller of Germany in 1953, of isometric contraction. It also recommended the regimen we were already using. Why, then, had we failed to make the promised gains? This was the question my friends took to York in 1962.

Upon their return I questioned them at length about isometric contraction, but the answers didn't satisfy me. Apparently the guys in York were training more or less as we were, and though I found the news depressing, my friends plunged back into their exercises with increased enthusiasm and with a growing tendency to look at one another in a knowing way during workouts and laugh out loud. Finally they showed me a small brown bottle that contained 100 five-milligram tablets of Dianabol. "This is the secret," they told me. "It's these little pink pills, not the isometric contraction." And so it was.

To learn how the York lifters and Hoffman got wind of isometric contraction—and anabolic steroids—we need to turn our attention to an unusual physician from rural Maryland, John B. Ziegler. Now retired and weakened by a variety of heart ailments, Ziegler was a big, robust man in the 1950s, full of good cheer and ideas about how to get strong. He knew the people at York, and in 1954 was the team physician for the U.S. weightlifters at the world championships in Vienna. "That was an important trip for me," he says. "I got to be friends with the Russian team doctor, and one night we went out on the town. We had a few drinks, and he told me some members of his team were using testosterone."

Back home, Ziegler learned from the medical literature that testosterone was first isolated in 1935 and that since then contraindications had accumulated as more and more animal and human studies were done. Though thus informed of some of the dangers inherent in the use of testosterone, Ziegler nonetheless decided to have a peek into Pandora's box. Conducting very limited case studies on several people, including himself, he found that although strength levels increased, so did the size of the prostate gland.

"Everyone got more 'studdy,'" he says. "The side effects were strong. Finally, in the late '50s, we got Dianabol, and it was about then that I read of the work that had been done in Germany on isometric contraction. It was in 1960 that I decided to try the steroids and the isometric contractions on a few of the top U.S. lifters, but I wish to God now I'd never done it. I'd like to go back and take that whole chapter out of my life.

"Steroids were such a big secret at first, and that added to the hunger the lifters and football players had to get hold of them. I honestly believe that if I'd told people back then that rat manure would make them strong, they'd have eaten rat manure. What I failed to realize until it was too late was that most of the lifters had such obsessive personalities. To them, if two tablets were good, four would be better."

The 35-year-old lifter who had been the first in my circle of acquaintances to use steroids recalls how he was introduced to them. "I first met Ziegler at the training camp for the Rome Olympics in 1960," he says, "and later that fall he invited me to come to his house in Maryland for a weekend. We spent several days talking about his ideas on isometric contraction and how they could be used to build strength in the Olympic lifts. He told me that two York lifters were already using a form of this training. He was such a great salesman that by the time the weekend was over I was ready to try it. He never said a thing about steroids then, but a week or so after I got home I got a letter from him and a bottle of pills. He told me they would help make sure I got the full nutritional value out of the food I ate. I was naive, I guess, but I'd never heard of Dianabol or steroids. I never questioned him, and from time to time I'd get a fresh supply. I was making great gains, and I thought the routine was doing it. In retrospect, though, I'm sure a lot of it was the pills."

In a number of predictable ways, the news of steroids spread. The combination of a radically different exercise routine, the startling progress being made by a small number of elite lifters, a wizardly physician and an evangelical promoter with access to a national fitness magazine produced a climate of rising expectations in which men of might began a big arms race, fueled by an ever expanding array of pharmaceuticals. This isn't to say that any one of these four components was individually responsible for the increased use of drugs in sport—only that these components happened to exist at the same time and to interact in such a way as to produce the critical mass necessary for the strength-building drug scene to explode. Ziegler and Hoffman are no longer really active in the game, the pacesetting lifters have all long since retired, and isometric contraction has acquired a patina similar to that of the bunny hop and the Hula-Hoop, yet the many and various ergogenic kin of Dianabol are thriving as never before.

In the last two decades steroid use has spread so far that it now causes only mild surprise when the athlete found guilty of having taken such drugs turns out to be a female middle-distance runner rather than a 300-pound male weightlifter. For example, a number of cyclists in the just completed Tour de France tested positive for steroids and were assessed time penalties. Among them was 1980 Tour winner Joop Zoetemelk of The Netherlands, whose use of the drug barred any hope of victory this time. But in the halcyon days of the early '60s, there were no women and only a few men who took steroids. And I was among them. *Mea gulpa.* My training partners, of course, were already taking them, and they urged me to begin immediately. But I was leery. Before I indulged, I at least saw an internist and took what precautions I knew to take. As I wrote in 1977, "I wanted to win, all right, and I wanted to win bad, but I wasn't stone crazy."

Just stone blind, at least to the extent of being unable to connect such terms as "enlarged prostate" and "liver toxicity"—phrases I encountered in the medical literature on steroids—to my own life. One thing often overlooked in discussions of the importance of educating young athletes about the potentially harmful side effects of steroids is that most young athletes, because of the effect their age and vigor have on their judgment, are almost constitutionally unable to hear such warnings. Reading *Thanatopsis* at 15 is, after all, an altogether different thing from reading it at 50.

So I took Dianabol intermittently from 1963 through early 1967, at which time I retired from competition. My best guess is that during the period I took approximately 1,200 pills, which would be 6,000 milligrams. When I tell young athletes these days of my dosage levels they look at me as if I were describing how margarine used to look during the Second World War, before the yellow coloring was added. Exactly how high the levels have gone is a matter of conjecture, but I have both testimony and published reports indicating that on occasion athletes have taken in less than two weeks the 6,000 milligrams that I, weighing more than 300 pounds, took in four years.

Looking back, I feel fortunate to have taken so few. Had the recommended dose been 10 times greater, I might well have taken it. In 1967 a doctor polled more than a hundred runners, asking them if they would take a certain drug knowing that, although it could make them Olympic champions, it could kill them in a year. More than half of the athletes responded affirmatively. *O tempora, O mores, oh hell.*

All of which is a way of saying that the various medical and sporting bodies concerned with athletics shouldn't be overly optimistic about the prospects of influencing the behavior of athletes by constantly stressing the capacity steroids have to produce unpleasant side effects.

As for the seriousness of the side effects, assessments of that depend to a large extent on your source. Some of the evidence is anecdotal, some is based on research data—although no research is available on subjects taking megadoses. Even so, the stance of such groups as the American College of Sports Medicine and the International Olympic Committee is, as one would imagine, research-based; their literature inveighs against the use of steroids and contains listings of potential deleterious side effects such as liver damage, decrease in testicular size and diminished sperm production. The ACSM adds, "Although these effects appear to be reversible when small doses of steroids are used for short periods of time, the reversibility of the effects of large doses over extended periods of time is unclear."

This statement, issued in 1977, is soon to be rewritten, and one of the men involved in doing research for the rewrite observes that most authorities in the field now feel that an ACSM claim made in 1977, that steroids did little, if anything, to enhance athletic ability, needs to be updated. The revised statement should take note of a flood of unofficial evidence and make some acknowledgment of what thousands of athletes have proved to their own satisfaction, which is that steroids, combined with proper training and nutrition, are able to produce athletic benefits, at least in the short run. What will also probably be changed is the section on risks, which will be expanded.

A sports scientist who has discussed the risks involved in steroid use is Capt. James Wright, Ph.D., a specialist in exercise physiology for the U.S. Army. In his recent book, *Anabolic Steroids and Sports, Volume II,* he observes, " . . . continually accumulating clinical and laboratory data indicate that dose and duration of use of oral anabolic and contraceptive steroids are the predominant factors influencing the development of hepatic lesions." He also notes that oral steroids have been increasingly implicated in the development of liver tumors, and continues:

"Conceivably, the use of anabolic hormones may lead to athero-sclerosis, hypertension, and disorders of blood clotting—the three major causes of heart attacks and strokes. The biochemical and physiological events and reactions which can ultimately lead to these effects have been observed in humans administered the drugs under clinical conditions as well as produced experimentally in various laboratory animals."

Thus it seems clear that athletes who use steroids are playing a risky form of roulette. The critical fact is that small doses taken for short periods is *not* the way most athletes are taking steroids. Because their effects are temporary, steroids must be in the system to be of benefit; once they are out of the system much of the strength they originally produced is lost. Here lies the problem. Athletes who make gains using steroids and hard training hate the idea of losing some of those gains, no matter how hard they may train, once they go off steroids. An additional difficulty, according to Wright and others, is that athletes tend to take ever larger dosages over longer periods of time. Thus the apparent increasing need of the body *for* steroids and the growing psychological dependence *on* steroids join hands to encircle the ambitious athlete.

One former athlete who understands this cycle is Dr. Craig Whitehead, a leading bodybuilder in the mid-1960s, who used steroids while competing. An ophthalmologist who now practices acupuncture in San Francisco, Whitehead for several years directed the drug rehabilitation unit of the Haight-Ashbury clinic. He is still involved in that field, and recently he said, "The dependence on steroids many people develop is classic. It's similar to that developed by people on so-called recreational drugs."

Another person who understands this problem with special poignancy is Larry Pacifico (SI, Aug. 6, 1979). Generally considered to have been powerlifting's premier performer, with a record nine consecutive world titles between 1971 and 1979, Pacifico barely escaped death 20 months ago from advanced atherosclerosis. He was 35 years old.

"One day in the fall of 1981 I was in the recovery room of a hospital following elbow surgery, and I had this terrible squeezing in my chest," he says. "The next morning they catheterized my arteries, and I learned that two arteries were approximately 70 percent blocked and one was almost completely closed—99.9 percent. I was immediately scheduled for a triple bypass, but they decided to try an angioplasty. It worked, but the whole experience has changed my life. I'm convinced my steroid use contributed to my coronary artery disease. I'm certain of it, and so is my doctor. I should have realized it was happening, because every time I went on a cycle of heavy steroid use I'd develop high blood pressure and my pulse rate would increase. Steroids aren't a part of my life now, but I'd be lying if I said I didn't miss them. And you know what? I may even take them again because I may not be able to *keep* myself from taking them."

Lest the last part of Pacifico's statement seem an isolated exaggeration, consider the fact that in the late '70s a high-ranking official of the U.S. Powerlifting Federation had a coronary bypass done, the need for which he blames at least in part on his use of steroids, yet he still took steroids for a later competition. Perhaps one of the ways this sort of mind-set can be explained is to examine the powerful effect that steroids—particularly testosterone—have on the central nervous system. Some researchers believe that even the anabolic steroids primarily work their magic not through the muscles themselves but through the central nervous system, by making the athlete feel energetic and aggressive, which leads to heavier and more intense training, which leads to improved performance. Whatever the truth of the preceding may be, there's no question that pure testosterone, particularly when used in large amounts, can have a pronounced effect on behavior.

The effect of hormones on personality is amply demonstrated by animal studies and electroencephalographic research carried out on humans. According to the limited testing done on human subjects, people given extra male hormones react in many of the same ways as people given amphetamines. Along with increased alertness, reduction in feelings of fatigue and mood elevation, however, go frequent and often extreme mood swings, such as those exhibited by some women with premenstrual syndrome. And it must be remembered that such psychophysiological changes have been produced by relatively small amounts of extra hormones.

Even though testosterone has been in use intermittently for almost 50 years, it only began to be taken with much regularity in the U.S. in 1977, when a few strength athletes in the amateur sports associated with the Olympic Games hit upon testosterone because, as a naturally occurring substance, it wasn't on the list of banned drugs, allowing athletes to beat the drug-testing procedures for anabolic steroids first used in 1976 at the Montreal Games. As these athletes experimented with testosterone they found that not only did it help to maintain their strength gains, it also made them feel tough as nails, confident and, as Dr. Ziegler says, "studdy." News spread fast, and soon other athletes in many sports were using testosterone. And it, of course, was using them.

One of the ways the old no-free-lunch lesson was learned by athletes who began to use testosterone was that as a group they began to suffer a great many more muscle and tendon injuries. Before its widespread use such injuries were rare among strength athletes, whereas now they are alarmingly frequent. Among lifters the two areas that tend to rupture are the biceps tendon and the quadriceps, the muscle on the front of the thigh. Since the widespread use of testosterone began, scores of men have either had the unpleasant experience of watching their biceps muscle roll up their arm like a windowshade after the tendon, at the point of its insertion into the bone of the forearm, gave way, or of collapsing to the platform after one or both of their quadriceps or patellar tendons ruptured. But although the increase in these injuries is not a matter of dispute, the reason, or reasons, for that increase aren't completely understood.

Some weight men argue that the injuries can all be attributed to the heavier poundages being lifted now. Others contend that because of the increased testosterone level something biochemical must happen to the muscle or tendon that makes it more brittle and likely to tear. Still others, and I lean toward their view, suggest that it can be explained by the aggressiveness produced by the testosterone, aggressiveness that causes the lifters to train hard when they should take it easy. This argument holds that the body normally tells an athlete when to back off, but the testosterone imperative to train hard and dominate the weights overrides these messages, with the result being injury.

Nor have the difficulties apparently stemming from the use of testosterone been only physical. The following matched pair of interviews were done at separate times, and the second interviewee hadn't seen the other's remarks. The subjects were at one time husband and wife. The man is nearing the end of a long career in football.

Wife: He's so impatient when he's on the steroids, so easily annoyed. He becomes vocal and hostile real fast, and he was never that way before.

Husband: It definitely makes a person mean and aggressive. And I was always so easygoing. On the field I've tried to hurt people in ways I never did before, especially if someone cheap-shots me. When they do I go for a death blow.

Wife: His sexual habits really changed. On the testosterone he not only wanted to have sex more often, he also was much rougher. And his sleep patterns were completely different on the testosterone. The Dianabol changed him some, but on the testosterone he was always ready to start the day by five-thirty or six, no matter how late he'd turned in. In the old days he'd sleep till noon.

Husband: One of the bad things about the testosterone is that you never get much sleep. It just drives you so. With amphetamines the effect wears off after a game, but with testosterone it's almost as if you're on speed all the time.

Wife: I don't think he'll ever be able to give it up. It cost him a wife who loved him and the chance to watch his two children grow up. There've been times when I felt he was almost suicidal. Sometimes, late at night, he'd tell me that he just couldn't help himself and that he couldn't stop using it because of the football, and then he'd cry.

Husband: I doubt if the NFL will ever try to stop it. The rule against it is just ignored now. But I've always told the doctors I was on testosterone, and nobody paid any attention.

Wife: The physical changes have been phenomenal. His skin has aged so fast, especially in the face—it's so much coarser now. And he lost his hair on top, right when he went on the steroids real heavy. But where in the past he didn't have much hair on his body, now his chest and back are covered, and the color of his genitals got darker. It was incredible.

Husband: A lot of guys can't handle it. I'm not sure I can. I remember a while back five of the guys on our team went on the juice at the same time. A year later four of them were divorced and one was separated. I've lost a lot of hair from using it, but I have to admit it's great for football. People in the game know that 50 percent of football is mental, and that's why the testosterone helps you so much. I lost my family, but I think I'm a better player now. Isn't that a hell of a trade-off? But the use of steroids in the NFL has grown steadily since I've been playing. I hear more and more talk about them.

Without adequate research conducted on subjects taking megadoses, it's impossible to clearly understand the potential steroids have for good or ill. One of the most extreme suggestions for cutting through the difficulties was put forth last fall in a speech by Arthur Jones, the founder, president and chief publicist of Nautilus Sports/Medical Industries Inc. At a strength-coaching conference at the University of Virginia, he announced the following grandiose plan:

"Next week I'm going south of the border to institute a 10-year study using thousands of subjects. Why south of the border? Because we can get the subjects at a price we can afford, and we can get subjects who are motivated, who will train. When you take starving subjects you can motivate them, believe me. We're going to take about 1,000 subjects and give them massive doses of steroids, and we're going to take another 1,000 and give 'em no steroids. You can't do that in this country. But you can do it down there. When they sign up for this program they'll be told in advance. 'Look, what we give you may be a drug, or it may not be. Even if it is, you won't know it. The drugs might be dangerous, and they might ruin your liver. Now if you don't want to sign up, there's the door, leave.'"

To date most of the money for research on steroids and athletics has been spent by the various bodies governing international amateur sports, particularly the IOC, in an attempt to develop testing procedures that would cut down on the taking of the drug before an event. The original tests, which could detect the presence of anabolic steroids in urine for a short time after they entered the body, were developed at Chelsea College and St. Thomas's Hospital, which are part of the University of London, by Professor Raymond Brooks and Dr. Arnold Beckett, among others. Essentially, the procedure involves a first screening of urine samples by means of radioimmunoassay. If the results of this indicate that an anabolic substance has been used, further tests using gas chromatography and mass spectrometry will reveal the type and the amount of the banned substances involved.

The procedure was first used in 1976 at Montreal, and six positive tests turned up. The offending athletes were disqualified. Over the next several years a number of other athletes came up positive, with perhaps the most celebrated case involving seven women, including three of the world's leading middle-distance runners, who were caught at European meets in 1979.

One reason more athletes weren't caught between 1976 and 1980 is that only a few sports pursued the tests with much vigor, and those few only at major competitions. (There are only six IOC-approved testing labs in the world, and the cost of testing is almost prohibitive.) Another factor curtailing the number of positive results is that when an announcement is made that a European track and field meet will have testing, assorted ailments break out among those who had planned to compete. And because rumor has it that a few of the athletes caught had been off steroids of all sorts for as long as three months, conservatism prevails.

But the factor that most fully explains the lack of more frequent positive test results in high-level sport is the "testosterone loophole." Before a major competition an athlete will stop taking the usual anabolic steroids while increasing his or her intake of testosterone. Because testosterone has both anabolic and androgenic effects, this allows the athlete to survive the testing with little, if any, loss of power. The loophole explains the otherwise puzzling fact that there was not even one positive test result for steroids at the Moscow Olympics. Unofficial urinalyses done by members of the IOC medical commission revealed, however, that 20% of the athletes, male and female, were probably using testosterone.

But now, partly because of those urinalyses, the testosterone loophole has been closed by the IOC. This comes as a relief to sports officials because the loophole resulted in two things, both of them bad. First, it made steroid testing, as previously administered, a joke. Second, the loophole implicitly encouraged athletes to switch from the anabolic steroids, considered to be comparatively benign, to testosterone, with all its capacity to virilize and increase aggression.

The first steps in closing the testosterone loophole were officially taken in early 1982 at the meeting of the medical commission of the IOC. Procedures to differentiate between endogenous, or naturally occurring, and exogenous testosterone and to establish limits of the former at a level that would prevent false positive test results had by then been developed. Thus the medical commission formally added testosterone to its long list of banned substances. By doing this, the commission removed one of the primary excuses used by various sporting federations, particularly in the U.S., to explain their reluctance to implement testing procedures at their major competitions. But although the IOC has mandated testing for testosterone at the next Olympics, the LAOOC is trying to reverse that decision for reasons that seem more political than scientific.

The Olympic Games are not the only place where the use of male hormones is a problem. Consider if you will the statement of a young man who was a scholarship athlete a few years ago at a state college in the eastern part of the U.S. "When we went to the dining hall we were given a paper cup with a bunch of pills in it," he said recently. "Most were vitamin pills of one sort or another, but there were 30 milligrams of anabolic steroids in there, too. And they chewed our butts if we didn't take everything. Still, that was mild compared to what I saw back home in New Jersey recently. I was at a local gym and this little black kid comes up to me with a bottle of pills in his hand and asks me what they are. They were Dianabol tablets, and when I asked him where he'd gotten them, he said his football coach had told him to go to the doctor and get some pills and take them. We all knew about that doctor, you could go to his office and without giving your age or taking any kind of a test, you could get a prescription for steroids. All you needed was the money. But at 14 years old?"

The standard justification of physicians like Robert Kerr of San Gabriel, Calif., who boasts of having more than 10,000 "patients" currently on steroids, is that since the people will use them anyway, prescriptions are safer. The same rationalization, of course, could be used for the prescribing of LSD and heroin.

But even without coaches or willing doctors, athletes can get steroids. The biggest sources are, in fact, not physicians but black-market dealers who sell the drugs illegally. Dr. Wright estimates that between 70% and 80% of the steroids taken in the U.S. are used not to heal the sick—the job they were intended to perform— but to strengthen the strong, and that of that 70% to 80%, between 80% and 90% are bought by athletes on the black market. Recently a few dealers decided that depending only on word of mouth to sustain sales just wasn't good enough. So, in the best tradition of American get-up-and-go, they began sending flyers to gym owners and other potential customers around the country. The flyers include a full price list of the available substances and complete details about how to order.

The question is: Now that it seems clear that steroids enhance performance, damage health and are readily available, how can athletes' use of them be curtailed? Sports organizations must begin by testing, in an attempt to force athletes to go off the drugs before major competitions. Few sporting bodies other than the IOC are concerned enough to do this.

TAC, which oversees track and field in the U.S., hasn't been very supportive of proposals from the International Amateur Athletics Federation medical committee to require IOC-type drug testing at any meet at which a world record is set. Indeed, TAC has never tested for drugs, and the reasons for that aren't easy to get at. Ollan Cassell, the executive director of TAC, flatly refuses to discuss the matter. Speculation centers on the notion that some TAC people may feel that they don't want to subject U.S. athletes to the sorts of regular testing, or even spot-check testing, that have been used so widely in Western Europe. This line of reasoning holds that since the Soviet bloc nations are unlikely to subject their athletes to such scrutiny, why should the U.S.? One result of this position is that it allows drug use among American athletes to escalate unchecked—hurdler Edwin Moses was quoted in June as saying that at least half of the top U.S. Olympic track and field candidates are using drugs, the most popular being anabolic steroids. This policy also calls into question how much TAC cares whether competition at its meets is really fair, and how much it cares about the health of its athletes. To their credit, many of the women in TAC do support testing.

In bodybuilding, a sport that has always prided itself on its dedication to good health, the Mr. America Committee of the AAU voted in 1982 to conduct a pilot study by requiring each of the 1983 AAU contestants in the U.S.A. series to have a drug test. Unforeseen logistical and legal hangups prevented this from happening, but the International Federation of Bodybuilders will conduct limited experimental testing this year in Europe. However, although the reaction against the influence of steroids in bodybuilding has prompted the AAU and the IFBB to act and spawned several so-called "natural" physique organizations, really bigtime bodybuilding is still test-free.

Though opposition to testing remains staunch among many of the top male bodybuilders, again there seems to be solid, though hardly universal, support for testing among the women competitors. Led by Doris Barrileaux, who serves as the IFBB women's committee chairperson, many of the women are urging the IFBB to begin to test immediately. "Bodybuilding is supposed to be healthy," Barrileaux says. "It's supposed to allow a woman to win without having to look like a man. I'd like to keep it that way."

And now we come at last to the sport I know best and am least objective about—powerlifting. Steroid use among athletes began at about the same time organized powerlifting did, and this sport's current efforts to deal with the issue of testing give particular insight into the difficulties involved.

Powerlifting lacks full affiliation with the IOC, and thus it has been free to establish its own rules. Until the U.S. Powerlifting Federation became independent, only last week, the sport had been part of the AAU, which for years has had an antidrug clause in its bylaws. But steroid testing wasn't a concern until the mid-'70s, when plans to test athletes at the Montreal Olympic Games were first discussed. At that time the use of drugs wasn't illegal in powerlifting, as no rules concerning them had ever been passed by the International Powerlifting Federation. But in 1977 it was decided that if powerlifting ever intended to join international federations such as the General Assembly of International Sports Federations or the IOC, it would be necessary to bring its rules more in line with those of the older and more prestigious organizations.

In 1978 legislation was passed by the IPF making the use of steroids illegal in powerlifting, but the rule was meaningless until 1982 because there was no provision for testing.

Although I retired as a competitor in powerlifting in 1967, in '71 my fascination with strength drew me back to the sport as a coach, a journalist and an official, and the first thing I noticed was the degree to which the level of drug use had soared. Beginning in '74 my interest increased, because my wife, Jan, decided to become a powerlifter, too.

When Jan first began to lift and for five years or so thereafter, she was often approached by friends who would suggest to her that she should give steroids a try, that they would really help her lifting. As she progressed in the sport—by 1977 she was setting records in every competition she entered—other friends began to ask what steroids she was taking and would, I think, only half believe her when she said she never used drugs. Following the first women's national level championships in '77, Jan began to assume more and more administrative responsibility in the sport.

In the late '70s Jan and I began to see more and more evidence—deepened voices and dramatic increases in upper-body strength and muscle size—that suggested some women were using steroids. Jan reacted to the shock of these startling transformations by strengthening her resolve not to use the drugs and to look for ways as an administrator to minimize their use in women's powerlifting. She was frightened by reports indicating that female rhesus monkeys given male hormones early in their pregnancies delivered female offspring that were dramatically abnormal. Their play was more aggressive, their clitorises were much enlarged and their labia majora were partially fused, as if to form a scrotal sac. Jan decided in her own case to fight the drugstore with the food store. In 1981 she reached a body weight of 230 pounds, at which she established a world record in the squat of

545.5 pounds, which still stands. Even though no official testing was then being done, Jan, on more than one occasion, insisted on urinalysis and a lie detector test to help make her desired point, that steroids aren't a necessity for world-class lifting.

At the end of the year, tired of shopping at the Lots To Love Shop, she decided she would quit competing for a while, lose weight and concentrate on her administrative duties. (She has since returned to competition, setting several world records in the 148-pound class.) It was at about that time that things began to heat up among U.S. powerlifters on the drug-testing question, in large part because of fires being lit here and there by Jan and the women's powerlifting committee, at least 90% of whose members favor testing. Last week the women lifters finally received the go-ahead to test for all steroids at their next national championships. Yet the same predominantly male committee approved only voluntary testing for those men who exceed current world records at the next men's national championships.

It's apparently in the nature of things for an adversarial relationship to develop between those entrusted with ensuring fair play and good health in a sport and those whose aim is to prevail. It didn't take athletes long to latch onto testosterone and to learn to time their anabolic steroid use and thus beat the tests. Now certain drug gurus smile knowingly about ways to evade any new net the testers may throw.

Rumors abound. One of the substances considered to be a hot ticket on the test-proof train these days is a powerful and frightening substance known as human growth hormone (HGH). A conservative three-week supply of the stuff has a street value of around $500, and the word now is that the only thing holding a lot of athletes back from using it is money. In the past, HGH had to be extracted from the pituitary glands of human cadavers, although our brave new world will soon have genetically engineered growth hormone available at a fraction of the current costs. The natural stuff is already widely used by elite athletes in the strength sports, and there apparently is no easy way to test for it.

Professor Beckett of Chelsea College and the IOC medical commission takes a balanced view of it all. "What we must always remember is this. It is a never-ending process. We can never eradicate drug use among athletes, but I think if we stay on our toes we can continue to develop procedures that will cause the athletes to use smaller amounts of drugs near the competitions, and this will promote fairness and health. That's our job. Consider the alternative."

Some people feel the current testing procedures and the will to enforce them are inadequate to the task of curtailing drug use in any meaningful way, and both body building and powerlifting have splinter organizations dedicated to using various types of lie detector tests to screen athletes. The largest of these is the American Drug Free Powerlifting Association. It has about 500 members and operates out of Bay St. Louis, Miss. under the direction of Brother Bennet of the Brothers of the Sacred Heart. Conversely, in powerlifting, some people have tried to start new federations with rules that would specifically forbid testing.

My own feeling, for what it's worth, is that the ergogenic aids an athlete chooses to use are his or her own business, up to a point. If a person wants to take 2,000 mg of anabolic steroids a day along with 3 cc of testosterone and say to hell with the risk-to-benefit ratio, I think that person should have the right to do so, outside official competitions. But after seeing what I've seen over the past five years or so; after hearing Jan console so many young girls, who call weeping to share with her the frustrations they feel as they face competition against women who have risked virilization and God knows what else to achieve the strength advantages conferred on them by the steroids; after seeing some of my friends wounded in body, in mind or both by steroid use; and after seeing many good people leave powerlifting because of their unwillingness to either take steroids or compete with the odds so against them, I think it's not unreasonable to tell those who wish to take steroids, "Look, use the drugs if you must, but don't stand in the way of reasonable drug testing in your sport. Either back off enough to be able to pass the IOC test at the big competitions or else stay out. Join another federation if you like, but you shouldn't expect the right to come in loaded against someone who's clean. If you wonder why, ask yourself why it would be unfair to begin a chess game with three queens to your opponent's one."

Over a year ago Jan wrote an ad hoc medical committee report recommending that testing be done at the forthcoming men's and women's national powerlifting championships. She stated the case well, I think. I hold with it.

"It is simply not fair," she wrote, "to allow one athlete to use a substance which both research data and empirical observation suggest is effective in producing significant strength gains, when a second athlete for medical and/or ethical reasons chooses not to use that substance. The nonuser of steroids has a right to expect the administrators of a sport to support policies which protect both fairness in competition and the good health of the athletes."

For taking the lead in efforts to establish drug testing in powerlifting for women, Jan has come under frequent attack, including attempts to have her removed as chairperson of the women's committee. One of powerlifting's problems is that it's a small sport, and most of the administrators in both men's and women's powerlifting are themselves competitors, which often puts those who must make decisions in a bind. People on both sides of the question have been intemperate, and people on both sides have, with cause, often felt wronged.

One of the proposed answers is to void any world records except those set in meets in which IPF-approved drug testing has been done. But who is to say how many men or women who have retired or suffered debilitating injuries would thereby lose a record they had set without the help of drugs? How can the organization justify taking a world record from those who did everything the IPF asked of them? No easy answers.

I have, however, heard world-record holders say they'd be willing to lose their records in support of a move toward testing. In a letter last winter to the IPF recommending that current world records be supplanted by lifts made in tested meets, Jan had this to say. "I will never again compete in the unlimited class, and so will never again have the chance to hold the squat or total record in that division if the IPF accepts our recommendation. I made great sacrifices in appearance when I increased my bodyweight to 105 kilos in order to lift those heavy weights, and I gained that weight because it was the only way I could remain competitive without taking steroids. I am certain that many powerlifters—

both men and women—use anabolic steroids for the same reasons I gained weight. We love the sport and we want to be winners. Many powerlifters to whom I've spoken feel trapped. They feel as if they have to break the basic rules of fair play and good health in order to compete. It could be argued that by not testing sooner the IPF is partly to blame for the extremely high level of some of the world records in our sport. Had we begun testing earlier, perhaps many men and women would have been spared the health risks, the expense and the ethical dilemma of steroid use.

"In any event, if we are now going to deny lifters the uninterrupted use of the very substances many of them took to create world records, we should in all fairness remove those records so that both the lifters who used drugs and those who didn't have a fighting chance to make new records. In my case, losing my world records is not nearly as important as helping to make powerlifting a fairer sport in which the health of our lifters is protected and in which *all* the world records represent lifts made in competitions with IOC testing."

I admire her so. I only hope my admiration does not diminish the seriousness with which the questions I have tried to raise—questions that range far beyond the small, perfervid world of powerlifting—will be taken. For seriousness is needed, especially as we move further into an era in which increasing numbers of athletes in all sports feel compelled to use drugs whose short-term effects are potentially harmful and whose long-range effects are largely unknown; an era in which the *Physicians' Desk Reference* is the bible of many world-class athletes; an era in which rumors circulate of "urine transfusions," by which a drug test is beaten by an athlete using a powerful diuretic, emptying his bladder, passing a catheter into his bladder through the penis and then receiving a supply of "clean" urine from someone into whom the opposite end of the catheter is inserted; an era in which fathers with large dreams for their small sons may turn to the soon-to-be-cheap human growth hormone in an attempt to give their boys a leg up; an era in which more and more photographs of top women athletes in a variety of sports reveal the thickly muscled, vein-crossed bodies that, though they do occur naturally on occasion in response to the stress of training, are often the result of the use of male hormones.

The hunger for an edge is an ancient one, intertwined with our need to excel. This hunger led me to take drugs I wish now I hadn't taken. So it goes. Have they had effects on me that will result in a shorter life? I don't know. I do realize that having taken them myself puts me in the position, when I try to discourage someone else from using them, of the old man whose opposition to the sexual activities of the young varies in inverse proportion to his own capacity to indulge. But having been under the dread sway of drugs myself and having reflected on the things I've done and felt and seen, it has seemed appropriate to share some of what I have learned about life in the Faust lane.

II. THE SPORTS INDUSTRY

EDITOR'S INTRODUCTION

The American public's appetite for sports entertainment is fed, for the most part, by television. Some 1,500 hours of sports events are poured onto the airwaves every year by the broadcast networks; cable networks and independent stations add thousands more. Because the audience is so vast, the profits from televised events are enormous. A sixty-second commercial aired during a national Football League game cost the sponsor $345,000 in 1984.

With so much money at stake, television has come to dominate the sports world, influencing everything from the formation of leagues to the scheduling of games. Even rule changes are made with TV in mind, as Larry Gerlach points out in his address from *Vital Speeches of the Day*. Still more pernicious, in Gerlach's view, is the effect of TV-dominated sports on social values—the priority given to victory at all costs, for example, and the glorification of athletic achievement beyond what is reasonable.

The next article in this section discusses the effects of television-dominated sports on the players themselves. Many professional athletes in popular team sports such as baseball, football, and basketball enjoy celebrity status and command multi-million-dollar salaries, a phenomenon analyzed by Robert Kilborn Jr. in an article from *Christian Science Monitor*. At the same time, however, athletes are under intense pressure to perform, and a growing number of them are resorting to drug and alcohol abuse, as Chass's article from *The New York Times* relates.

In the last article in this section, reprinted from the *Atlantic*, sociologist Harry Edwards discusses another aspect of sports-for-profit: the corruption of intercollegiate athletics, with its disastrous results for the young athletes who receive no education from colleges for whom they play and who are unemployable after they graduate.

TELECOMMUNICATIONS AND SPORTS[1]

Before I begin my remarks, I would like to let you know where I am coming from in terms of interest in sports. I was on my way to Cooperstown by way of the New York Yankees when I discovered as a freshman at the University of Nebraska that I could no longer throw or hit a curve ball. I then bent upon a career in football and I was going to play, believe it or not, with the Detroit Lions. Except as a freshman at the University of Nebraska, I got hurt. I was not injured, I was only hurt. People kept beating the hell out of me, and I decided that what I would then do is turn to history.

I always had an interest in sport but it was not considered to be academically respectable in those days. When I got to the University of Utah, intent on staying a year or two—that was fifteen years ago—I got involved with the athletic program, was a member of the athletic board for some eight years and began at that time to very seriously cultivate an interest in understanding sport as a social, political, and economic phenomenon in our society.

My remarks today will constitute remarks, not a paper. I wrote a paper three weeks ago on television and intercollegiate sports and then when the program for this symposium arrived I realized that there was a session devoted to that so I tore it up and wrote another paper. A couple of days ago I had a fight with my son about sports and I wrote another paper. What I did this weekend, is take parts of the three papers and put them together, the idea being that I would not try to present any kind of definitive statement about sport but rather throw out a number of ideas that we might discuss.

Each spring I teach a course entitled, "The History of Sport in America." The course draws extremely well with 300 or 400 students. It is the only course I teach where the students come con-

[1]Excerpted from an address entitled "Telecommunications and Sports: The Future of Sports in American Society," by Larry Gerlach, professor of history, University of Utah. *Vital Speeches of the Day.* 50:345–8. Mr. 15, '84. Reprinted by permission of the author from *Vital Speeches of the Day.* Copyright © 1984 Larry Gerlach.

vinced of the importance of the subject at hand and are deeply interested in exploring the topic at great length.

The first day of class I ask two questions: What is sport? What is athletics? I am not especially bothered when most students respond to my questions by casting their eyes downward in the unmistakable, 'please don't call on me' message of body language. But I am perplexed that without exception my students who cover sports for the local campus newspaper have no idea as to the nature of that about which they write. And I am absolutely amazed that the 40 or 50 varsity athletes in class have no intellectual comprehension of the activity which brought them to the university in the first place and which constitutes the driving force of their collegiate lives.

Sport, I am convinced, is the best known yet least understood phenomenon in American society. Much of our misunderstanding and misconceptions about sports stems from our failure to make meaningful distinctions among the various components of sport world. And I don't want to get into a long definitional discussion here, except to highlight the difference between our two major sports phenomena.

One is sport. Sport is an extension of play involving two or more persons. Sport turns on games and contests which are highly organized, competitive, characterized by the established rules, but like play, sport has as its primary purpose fun for the participant.

Athletics on the other hand, derives not from play at all, but from work. Athletics as they have been referred to from the ancient Greeks on, refers to intensely competitive confrontation between especially trained performers whose primary objectives are: a) spectator entertainment and b) victory. Although the game involved in sport and athletics may be the same, as, for example, basketball, the two activities are worlds apart in terms of purpose and attitude. And to make this very complicated thing exceedingly simple, I would simply call your attention to the obvious difference that we understand between intramural sport and intercollegiate athletics.

My reason for raising the definitional issue is not to confuse but to clarify. The fundamental truth is that modern, American society is preoccupied not with sport but with athletics. This symposium is in fact misnamed; the telecommunications industry is interested in athletic contests, not sporting events. However, today I will defer to convention and use sport and athletics interchangeably.

Two fundamental and basically irreconcilable philosophical conflicts color our involvement with sport. First of these is that while we extol the amateur sportsman we insist that our performers be professional athletes. Second, we want sport to be fun and to be purposeful. Now the amateur/professional dichotomy we can talk about later if you'd like. Today, in trying to determine the sort of role or why the emphasis on sport in American society, I would like to look at that second phenomenon.

Purposeful sport; although we persist in paying lip service to the fun or the recreational dimension of sport, the historical record clearly shows that Americans have always considered sports to be primarily a serious, that is, a purposeful activity. The roots for purposeful play extend deep into our past: to the inability of New England Puritans to distinguish between work and play; to the efforts of pre–Civil War reformers and child guidance writers to promote sport as a means of developing ethical values and character traits, discipline, courage, teamwork necessary for success in a modernizing society; to the attempts of the late 19th century to utilize sport as a means of Americanizing immigrants, controlling the frustrations of industrial laborers and ensuring the physical fitness of a virile nation on the global make; and to the recent systematic efforts of the government to employ sport as the mechanism of chauvinism, military preparedness, and international diplomacy.

Surely our emphasis on sport in modern America stems in large measure from the basic fact that Americans view sport as a serious, purposeful, enterprise related to the fundamental well-being of society at large. We still hear, and this is why I had a fight with my son, ad nauseam, such mindless prattling as "sport builds character" when the very actions of the lords of sport give lie to that simpleminded rhetoric.

What is the larger significance of our insistence on purposeful sport? I would like to quote to you and then comment on two observations, one from a student of American culture and another from a sports writer. The first, the student of American culture, Christopher Lasch, who wrote an issue entitled, "The Corruption of Sport." And Chris Lasch made this observation:

The degradation of sport consists in its subjugation to some ulterior purpose, such as profit making, patriotism, moral training or the pursuit of health. Sport may give rise to these things in abundance but ideally it produces them only as by-products having no essential connection with the game.

And second is Robert Lipsyte, former sports writer for the *New York Times*:

For the past 100 years most Americans have believed that playing and watching competitive games are not only healthful activities but represent a positive force on our national psyche. This faith in sport has been vigorously promoted by industry, the military government and the media. The values of the arena and the locker room have been imposed on our national life. Even for ball games these values with their implicit definitions of manhood, courage, and success are not necessarily in the individual's best interest, but for daily life they tend to create a dangerous and grotesque web of ethics and attitudes. The sport experience has been perverted into a sport world state of mind in which the winner was good because he won and the loser, if not actually bad, was at least reduced and had to prove himself over again through competition (i.e. Roberto Duran). Sport World is a grotesque distortion of sport, it limits the pleasure of play for most Americans while concentrating on turning our best athletes into clowns. It makes the finish more important than the race.

Well, among modern students of sport and society, terms like corruption, distortion, grotesque, and degradation are watchwords. Surely these are among the by-products of purposeful sport in America today.

The problems associated with purposeful sport have always been with us, but as we have moved during the past three centuries from informal folk games and recreations before the Civil War to organized commercial sport after the Civil War to the era of national sport industries today, those problems have been increasingly troublesome. Just as television is responsible for the creation of the modern sport industry, television has contributed fundamentally to the problem of modern sport. The impact of television is manyfold.

First of all, promotional. The enormous capacity of television to reach people has sold sport. If TV moguls devote so much programming time to sport, then sport must be important. If television devotes virtually an entire day to covering the Super Bowl, then that contest must be important. And by extension, sport itself must be very important. I would suggest that sport is regarded as being much more influential in our society than it really is because of the attention that television pays to it.

The second is financial. Television with its national marketing capabilities has brought unbelieveable wealth to the world of sport and created nothing short of a sport industry. The result has been an extraordinary proliferation of sport franchises and leagues—the major leagues, baseball, the National Football League, the NBA. When I was a kid, that is in the 1950's, there was no resemblance to these institutions today. The result is greatly expanded playing schedules and the domination of sport not by the gentlemen sportsmen of the pre-WWII era, but by corporate executives. Once there was a Tom Yawkey and now there is a George Steinbrenner. It is often said—it is a cliche—that money is the root of all evil and so it is with the world of sport.

Television, third, has fundamentally intruded on sport by directly affecting the contests themselves. Baseball's league championship series and night-time World Series, football's absurd playoffs, and the hyperbolic Super Bowl, even NCAA's utterly reprehensible mass post-season basketball tournament is due to television payoffs. Contests start at times that conflict fundamentally with common sense and the interest of performers because of television payoffs. My friend, Bear Bryant, says "I'll play anytime, anywhere, if the price is right." Basketball now incorporates TV time-outs in a way that fundamentally affects the strategy and execution of the game. The New York Jets defeated the San Diego Chargers earlier this season thanks in part to a referee's concern about a TV commercial. Two-minute warnings in professional football games are there simply to provide one more commercial opportunity. The point is that television does not merely broadcast games; television manipulates the games.

Fourth, television broadcasts a distorted image of sport. Television promotes an illusion of sport, its values, its importance, its role in society, that is at odds, I think, with reality. Television is not concerned with sport but with professional athletics. Television made the National Football League. Television made the National Basketball Association. Television made the golf and professional tours. At the time of WWII, there was no stable NFL, there was no systematic professional basketball in this country, there was no golf tour, there was no tennis tour. And today when most Americans think of sport they think of professional televised sport. And it is not surprising, I think, that the sports that are televised are the ones that televise best. The coverage of sport in your local newspaper is a far more accurate view of Americans' interest in sport than the broadcast schedules of the national networks. Although I keep complaining about the coverage in my local paper, the sports editors know the real world of sport.

Fifth, television promotes a perverse concept of the professional athlete as the norm in sport world. The pros have become the models and the values of the pro game become the values of the sport generally. I think that is obvious to anyone who has watched youth or high school sports and those youngsters slavishly imitating the pros. The athlete is a conspicuous minority among the inhabitants of the sport world, yet the athlete sets the tone due to television. Moreover, the incredible hype of television promotes a larger than life concept of sport in which winning triumphs over participation.

Do not under-estimate sport think, which has fundamentally and, I think, cruelly defined my son's self-image and his world view. Now, as to the future of this, the pro games will go on albeit in somewhat diminished form. I think we can put up with only so much shlock, so much pimping, so much hype, and frankly so much bull. Ratings are down for Monday night football whether it is Monday Night Football on Monday, Monday Night Football on Wednesday, Monday Night Football on Thursday, Monday Night Football on Friday, Monday Night Football on Saturday or Monday Night Football on Sunday. Television has made sport almost a caricature, a grotesqueness of cheap commercialism where the broadcast all too often overshadows the contest. Monday Night Football is only the most gross offender. The likelihood is that network coverage will diminish in favor of cable broadcasting, which focuses more closely on the contest per se.

The greatest impact of television has been on intercollegiate athletics. Television in the next decade promises to accomplish what university presidents, athletic directors and coaches have been trying to do for the last 100 years, namely, destroy intercollegiate athletics as an academic amateur sports enterprise. The open professionalism of intercollegiate athletics will, if nothing else, end the rampant corruption and blatant hypocrisy that currently afflict the collegiate sport establishment.

In 1873, Andrew D. White, president of Cornell University, responded thusly to a request by Cornell footballers to travel to Michigan for a game. "I will not permit thirty men to travel 400 miles merely to agitate a bag of wind." Three years later John Bascom, President of the University of Wisconsin, responding to student and alumni pressure for increased athletic programs as entertainment, said, "If athletics is needed for amusement, we should hire a few persons as we do clowns to set themselves apart to do this work."

Well, in the intervening years, university presidents learned about the money to be made from intercollegiate sport—if not directly, then indirectly through alumni donations and so on—and 100 years later, my friend, Bear Bryant, made the following statement: "I used to go along with the idea that football players on scholarships were student athletes which is what the NCAA calls them, meaning a student first, an athlete second." We are, of course, kidding ourselves trying to make it more palatable to the academician. We don't have to say that anymore and we shouldn't. At the level we play, the boy is really an athlete first and a student second. When men like Joe Paterno of Penn State and Tom Osborn of Nebraska agree to play a kickoff classic in August in East Rutherford, New Jersey, after publicly arguing that the game was against the best interest of the program and their players, the collegiate sport scene is in sad shape.

Well, I ducked the basic issue here which is the great appeal of sport today and I wrote some remarks which are intended to be provocative. And I wrote them after watching a Lite Beer commercial which kind of puts the whole thing together. Two famous football players, trying to achieve a modicum of class and culture, have gone to the opera. Well, I wonder why the great appeal of sports today. I think it is very simple. Sport accurately reflects American society, its frustrations, its fantasies, its cultural values. The arena is at once apart from and a part of everyday life. But, of course, the same thing is true for a variety of other activities, i.e., the opera, so what is the special appeal of sport? My son asked me about the comment he hears always that sport is simply children's games played by adults. He said, "Is that right?" And I think that is right and I think that is why sport plays such a very important role in our society.

Four reasons: Sport is pure. That is, sport is the only non-ideological cultural activity in our society, or any society. Literature, art, music, dance, all of these activities are value-laden. Sport is only a kinetic enterprise. There is no value represented as two athletes line up to run 100 meters. It is pure. It is innocent. It is basic.

Second, sport is elemental and elementary. It involves confrontation between obvious good guys—my team, and obvious bad guys—your team. That conflict is cleanly, finely, and clearly resolved through the use of physical force. The more physical the game, the more popular the game. One defeats opponents literally by beating them and that is the basic mechanism of conflict resolution. It is, in a word, kind of Star Wars mentality.

The third, sport is simple and simplistic. It is the cultural activity in our society that is wholly intelligible to the lowest common denominators in society. My thirteen-year-old can discuss basketball on an equal basis with me. It is the ideal cultural activity in a democracy, rather like the public school system. It is intelligible, too, and embraceable by all elements in the culture.

And fourth, sport, to continue the childhood metaphor, is fantastic. That is, sport turns on illusion, on fantasy, on dreams, whether dreams of future glory or nostalgic remembrances of glories that once were or might have been. I think it symbolic that the relationship between journalism, particularly broadcast journalism, and sport is so evident and that the majority of TV addicts, Star Wars freaks, fairy tale fanatics and sports fans in this country are children. Sport represents in large part the maintenance of childlike innocence and values in a harsh, cynical adult world.

Speaking of kids, to wind up my formal remarks, whatever the reality of sport and sport personalities, in my youth there were perceived heroes, perceived exalted values to sport participation. That's why I ate and slept and breathed sport. As a youth, I viewed sport as a blissful refuge from everyday life. Today my son views sports as a component of the cheapness, tackiness, selfishness, corruption of everyday life. The tragedy is that where I once believed, my son and his friends have never believed. Fantasy has always been an essential, perhaps the essential, element in sport. If sport loses its illusions and becomes part and parcel of reality, I fear very much about the future of sport in American society.

TRYING TO LIMIT OUT-OF-THE-BALLPARK SALARIES IN PROFESSIONAL SPORTS[2]

Wealth doesn't weigh heavily on Dave Winfield's broad shoulders.

"I live well—like I'm probably entitled to," he says pleasantly.

A New York Yankee outfielder of considerable talent, Mr. Winfield is sipping a soft drink amid the din of the visitors' clubhouse before a game at Boston's Fenway Park. He is reflecting on the high salaries paid to professional athletes—a trend that has made him and a growing number of other sports pros very comfortable financially.

"The sport can handle it," he says. "There is extra money in the game. It's just a matter of how they allocate the money and what they want the individual to do to earn that money." . . .

Multi-million-dollar salaries used to be the exclusive preserve of movie stars and captains of industry. No longer. Now those who can run, jump, throw, catch, or hit better than their peers can command what is known in the business world as "serious money."

[2]Excerpted from a newspaper article by staff writer Robert Kilborn Jr. *Christian Science Monitor.* p 1+. Je. 28, '83. Copyright © 1983 by The Christian Science Publishing Society. Reprinted by permission from *The Christian Science Monitor.* All rights reserved.

Noted Boston sports attorney Bob Woolf, who has negotiated 1,800 contracts for athletes, says, "As ridiculous as salaries] seem now, they're going to go higher."

Adds Upton Bell, one of the nation's best-known radio sports talk-show hosts and a former pro football executive: "The situation will not stop until the same thing hits sports that hit the auto industry.

"Our entertainment demands are highest during times of stress," he maintains, referring to such ordeals as the Vietnam war and the recent recession. "And the less we have to do, the more we're going to watch."

The battle for viewers (and advertising) between network and cable television is expected to enrich professional sports for years to come—providing teams with added capital to invest in players.

Last year the National Football League (NFL) accepted a five-year, $2 billion contract with the three major commercial TV networks. Because of the pact, each of the league's teams will automatically receive $13 million a year. This spring, major-league baseball approved a six-year, $1.1 billion deal with ABC and NBC beginning in 1984—over and above the value of local TV and radio contracts.

Cable TV's growth has been uneven so far. But by the National Cable Television Association's projections it will increase from 32 million US households now—or 38 percent of all TV households—to 55 million (or 58 percent of projected TV households) by 1990. Already cable companies are involved in the ownership of professional teams, notably baseball's Pittsburgh Pirates and Atlanta Braves.

To the dismay of many fans and nonfans alike, meanwhile, the cavernous salary gap between those who play sports for a living and those in more conventional occupations is growing wider.

Whereas a public-school teacher or police officer may not hope to earn more than $30,000 a year:

• Winfield, of the Yankees, has a 10-year contract with the team worth an estimated $25 million—he claims the actual value "is much greater than has been published"—and says: "I would hope I'd be making double what I'm making now by the time I finish the game."

• Los Angeles Lakers center Kareem Abdul-Jabbar is the object of a bidding war among National Basketball Association (NBA) teams that will likely push him into the $2-million-a-year bracket. Boston Celtics forward Larry Bird also is a candidate for a $2-million-a-year contract.

Even at that level, they wouldn't be as highly paid as Moses Malone, who recently led the Philadelphia 76ers to the 1982–83 NBA championship. Mr. Malone accepted a six year, $13 million offer from the 76ers last fall. Not counting his share of the playoff money, he earned an estimated $2.97 million in salary and bonuses for the season just ended.

• Running back Herschel Walker left college in his junior year last winter to sign with the New Jersey Generals of the United States Football League (USFL) at a reported $4.8 million for three years.

• John Elway, the All-America quarterback from Stanford University, last month agreed to a $1-million-a-year contract with the Denver Broncos of the NFL—a league record.

The inflated salary structure even applies to head coaches and field managers, once expected to work for modest salaries while trying to coax championship performances out of their higher-priced athletes. Billy Cunningham of the Philadelphia 76ers has just agreed to a new contract that will pay him an estimated $400,-000 a year.

"There will always be a great imbalance [between athletes' salaries and those in other occupations]," says Upton Bell. "For as many people who might be jealous, there are just as many who say, 'Hey, more power to 'em!'"

Recently a Boston newspaper polled readers on the merits of paying the Celtics' Bird what he wants. Respondents spiced their replies with such comments as, "Nobody is worth $2 million," and "$2 million equals 40 teachers at $50,000 per year." But 85 percent of them wished to see Bird remain in a Celtics uniform even at that price.

Says Herb Escot of the Center for Sport and Social Issues at Northeastern University in Boston: "All of the teams' assets are players. Take away the players and what have you got? A few desks. They're simply taking their revenues and distributing them among their assets."

What these salaries have wrought, however, is a subject of endless controversy. Huge contracts are no guarantee of success on the field or court. And when teams fail to perform as expected, fans often turn on the owners and the owners sometimes turn on their players.

Baseball players have declined the opportunity to play for the prestigious New York Yankees because of owner George Steinbrenner's reputation for criticizing his employees in public for not winning.

There also appears to be substantiation for the claim that many highly paid athletes pamper themselves at the first sign of illness or injury. Ken Lehn, an economist at the Washington University School of Business in St. Louis, recently found a 165 percent increase in the number of days that major-league baseball players spent on the disabled list after signing contracts that guaranteed their salaries whether they played or not. Using 1980 as the base season, Dr. Lehn found that players with at least three years remaining on their contracts averaged 79 percent more time on the disabled list than those with one or two years left.

Some attempts are being made to come to grips with the spiraling salaries. Beginning with the 1984 season, most NBA teams will be bound by a $3.6 million total payroll cap, in agreement with the league players' union. Thus, if a team owner agrees to pay one player, say, $2 million, the remaining 10 players on his roster will have to divide $1.6 million.

The cap increases to $4 million for 1986, when the agreement expires. Teams already over the limit may remain over, but may not sign free agents or trade for additional players who would increase their payrolls.

COCAINE DISRUPTS BASEBALL FROM FIELD
TO FRONT OFFICE[3]

Cocaine use among baseball players has been so pervasive in recent years that the drug's debilitating effects have tarnished individual performances, shortened careers and influenced the outcome of games and pennant races, club officials and players say.

John McHale, president of the Montreal Expos, said cocaine was the reason his team did not win its division championship in 1982, when the team generally was considered to be the best in the National League.

"I don't think there's any doubt in '82 that whole scenario cost us a chance to win," McHale said. "We felt we should've won in '82. When we all woke up to what was going on, we found there were at least eight players on our club who were into this thing. There's no question in my mind and Jim Fanning's mind—he was managing the club that year—that cost us a chance to win."

Executives and managers also acknowledge that cocaine has become a major factor in trade talks and has made managers suspicious when they see players make mistakes on the field.

Although people involved in the game have been reluctant to assess the impact cocaine has had on baseball, a three-month investigation by The New York Times found that the subject is one that players and club officials have thought much about, in part because of growing evidence of extensive cocaine use among players. In a series of interviews marked by unusual candor, several members of each group agreed to discuss their experiences and conclusions.

Players Describe Effect

Two top players who underwent drug rehabilitation, Tim Raines of the Montreal Expos and Lonnie Smith of the Kansas

[3]Reprint of an article based on reporting by Murray Chass and Michael Goodwin and written by Mr. Chass. *New York Times*. A 1, B 8. Ag. 20, '85. Copyright © 1985 by The New York Times Company. Reprinted by permission.

City Royals, told how the drug adversely affected their play. Smith told of hiding his cocaine in pockets in his socks; Raines told of carrying cocaine in gram bottles in his uniform pants pocket and of using it between innings in the restroom behind the dugout.

In 1982, the Expos finished in third place, six games from first in the National League's East Division. Raines, who the season before had established a major league record for stolen bases by a rookie, was one of the players McHale belatedly discovered was using cocaine.

'I'd Start Arguing'

"It certainly hurt my performance," said Raines, a 25-year-old outfielder, who underwent addiction treatment after the 1982 season. "I struck out a lot more; my vision was lessened. A lot of times I'd go up to the plate and the ball was right down the middle and I'd jump back, thinking it was at my head. The umpire would call it a strike and I'd start arguing. He'd say, 'That ball was right down the middle.' When you're on drugs, you don't feel you're doing anything wrong."

The question of how cocaine affects baseball is a complex one, if only because success in the major leagues is difficult to achieve and depends on many factors. The history of the game is filled with stories of promising youngsters who failed to achieve stardom, or even mediocrity, and of established players who suddenly, without explanation, lost their abilities. Sometimes, alcohol has been cited as the villain and, sometimes, unspecified "off the field" problems have been blamed. Cocaine is the latest factor in the formula, different if for no other reason than it is illegal.

Moreover, the effects of cocaine can vary, depending on when, how much and how often an individual uses it. The effects can be dramatic if a player uses it just before or during a game. If a player restricts his use to non-game times and uses it only occasionally, there could be little or no effect, doctors say. For those who use cocaine regularly but not on the field, the effects might show up gradually.

"There is no doubt in my mind that the stimulant does improve performance but it is short-lived," said Dr. Howard S. Rubin, who has studied the drug's effect on athletes as president and clinical director of the California Institute for Behavioral Medicine. "After a brief time, it becomes destructive."

Questions about Use Arise
in Trade Talks

A government source in Pittsburgh, where at least 11 active players, including Raines and Smith, and one former player testified before a grand jury, said a common tale told by players there was that they had a good game after using cocaine for the first time, then kept using it in the belief that it helped their performance. However, they eventually discovered that the drug hampered them and diluted their talent.

Perhaps the clearest example could be that of Willie Wilson, who was one of four Kansas City players imprisoned after the 1983 season on cocaine charges. Although Wilson said the issue of the drug's effect on his performance was irrelevant because he never used it during games, his .332 batting average that won the American League batting title in 1982 plummeted to .276 in 1983, the only time he has batted under .300 in the six seasons he has been a regular in the Royals' outfield.

John Schuerholz, general manager of the Kansas City Royals, stopped short of blaming cocaine for the team's failure to win the American League West title in 1982, when the team finished three games from first. The Royals learned later that several of their starting players had been using cocaine regularly.

"It's so hard to isolate the effect the problem had on the club," Schuerholz said. "We didn't win the pennant. We did have a drug problem. But that's not to say we could've won if we hadn't had the problem. I don't know if we would have won without the problem. But we've always challenged for titles."

Whitey Herzog, who took over a last-place team when he became the St. Louis manager in mid-1980, said that perhaps 40 percent of his players were using cocaine at the time. Asked what effect it might have had on their play, he said pointedly, "We were dead last when I got here."

One owner, who asked not to be identified, said he understood that use was especially prevalent among relief pitchers. If the owner's understanding is correct and those pitchers use cocaine during games, it would fit the pattern described by doctors who say the drug can give a user a 45-minute high. That stimulant would be enough to carry a relief pitcher through perhaps three innings.

It is easy, of course, for clubs to keep track of the players who have undergone rehabilitation. It is not so easy for them to know which players are users when the clubs become involved in trade talks with other teams.

Bill Giles, president of the Philadelphia Phillies, said possible drug use is a subject of immediate interest in trade talks. "That's one of the first things clubs ask," he said. "Is he healthy and is he clean?"

Or there is the approach noted by Tom Haller, general manager of the San Francisco Giants: "What you ask is whether this guy takes care of himself. I guess that's one way of asking if he's clean."

Schuerholz said that trades often are not made because of a suspicion of drug use. "I've heard people say on a lot of occasions, 'I won't involve myself with this guy because I've heard of this or that,'" Schuerholz said.

Dick Howser, the Royals' manager, added, "You probably spend as much time researching that as you do finding out about whether a guy can bunt or hit-and-run."

Murray Cook, general manager of the Expos, said clubs "try to get as much information as you can on anybody."

Cook also talked to the problem of sifting through and investigating the rumors. "That's happened with a lot of players," he said. "They've been painted with a brush. It's such a nebulous area, trying to determine whether or not a player is involved with drugs. It's easy to generalize. It's easy to say this player is performing in such a fashion, he's got to be using drugs. The drug situation is pretty unpredictable. It's hard to tell who's involved, who isn't. You've got to be very careful. It makes it very difficult."

The issue also creates difficulties for players. Chili Davis, a Giant outfielder, was one of four players on the current San Francisco team mentioned by a former Giant as having used cocaine in recent years. "I tried it before," Davis acknowledged. "It wasn't for me. It made my body deteriorate. It made me feel bad. The day after I tried it, I felt drained."

Davis, who had his worst season in 1983, said that he was approached by both the Federal Bureau of Investigation and Giants coaches that season. "The coaches," he said, "whisper, 'Hey, they think you're on cocaine. You're not getting mad when you make outs any more.'"

Davis said he stopped using the drug after being approached by the F.B.I. But some of the suspicion lingered.

Davis said, "Last year, an ex-player came up to me and said, 'They got you; they're watching you.' I said, 'What are they watching me for?'"

Nothing, though, was more difficult for the Expos than the discovery that cocaine had undermined their efforts a few years ago.

"It slipped in the back door and you didn't even know it was in the house," McHale said sadly.

Raines, the rookie sensation, was the only member of the 1982 Expos publicly identified as a cocaine user. He voluntarily entered a treatment center after the season. "Now that I look back," Raines said not long ago, "I probably was the only one that did undergo treatment, but I wasn't the only one that needed to."

McHale said some of the Montreal cocaine users "seemed to be so far gone" that the Expos didn't try to rehabilitate them. Raines, he said, "worked hard" at his rehabilitation.

"He probably cost us six, eight, 10 games doing things we couldn't believe he was doing," McHale said of the outfielder. "We moved him to second base for a while and there were times he held the ball without making a play. He'd be on first base and he couldn't run; they picked him off. He couldn't find balls in the outfield. After we found out what was wrong, we said why couldn't we spot it? You look for excuses, like maybe there's too much pressure on him, or maybe he has problems at home."

Raines said he became involved with cocaine through older teammates. He wouldn't discuss his testimony in Pittsburgh or identify any of his teammates who were involved with him, but added, "When I got anything, it was always from a player." Over all, he said he used the drug with "eight or nine" players, mostly teammates but also some players from other teams.

Raines described himself as a "sort of quiet guy" when he arrived in the major leagues in 1981. "I never knew what drugs were when I was growing up," he said. "Once I got into the big leagues, you just sort of want to fit in. I felt it was just an experiment I tried, and I got hooked. You can't just turn it on and off that easily. I just got in with the wrong people."

Raines said he never found it difficult to get cocaine. "Anytime there's a big party, there's going to be drugs around," he related. "That's the easiest thing to do, to meet someone."

Parties and players and cocaine seem to be a popular combination. When players attend parties, other people often want to ingratiate themselves with these stars by giving them whatever they want.

Ron Davis, a relief pitcher with the Minnesota Twins, recalled how, when he played for the Yankees, he and teammates would go to parties in New York. "I have seen a lot of cocaine around, not that any of our players took it," Davis said. "But it was there if you needed it. A guy would come up to you and say, 'Let's go into the back room. I got some stuff.' He was giving it to us for free if we wanted it. Some of us left. We didn't want to get blamed for using it."

Sliding Head First to Protect
His Cocaine

Raines, on the other hand, used—and used and used. During the 1982 season, he said, he had three months of particularly heavy use, using cocaine virtually every day. But he was careful about where he bought the drug.

"You're taking a chance as an athlete to try to obtain some and risk it being an undercover agent," he said. "I never went out and sought to get it from someone on the street. I never had the guts to do it. When I got anything, it was always from a player."

It didn't take Raines long to become a regular user.

"You find yourself liking it," he said. "You try it again and again. All of a sudden, it gets to the point where you have to have it. It's like an upper. You come down, you feel sluggish, sick. When you're high, you feel normal, but it's not really normal."

Players don't normally take naps in the dugout between innings either, but Raines at times did just that, being exhausted from staying up late using cocaine.

In 1982, Raines did not have what for him was a normal season. His average dropped 27 points to .277; he drove in only six more runs in more than twice as many times at bat as he had the previous season and he struck out nearly three times as often. He also had only seven more stolen bases than he had the year before in the strike-shortened season. In 1981, he stole one out of every 1.97 times he reached base; in 1982, he stole one out of every 3.26 times.

Raines said he often went into the bathroom behind the dugout to use more between innings. Where did he keep it?

"I had it in little gram bottles that I kept in my pocket," he related. "Actually, a lot of times, I would put it in my batting glove and then in my pocket. I was trying to find ways of not getting caught." When he slid into a base, Raines added, he was sure to protect his investment. "Usually," he said, "when I carried it in my pocket, I'd go in head first."

Delivering Cocaine by Federal Express

Lonnie Smith, who said he used cocaine for several years, was another player who took great care to protect his stash. A heavy user when he played the outfield for the St. Louis Cardinals in 1983, Smith told of the different ways he concealed his supply.

"The majority of the time, I hid it on me," he said. "I had these Playboy socks with pockets in them and I'd stick it in there. I had ways of folding my clothes, 10, 12 pairs of pants in a suitcase. I learned it from a Latin friend in Venezuela. People who wanted to check wouldn't take the time."

During the offseason, he said, he and his supplier had a simple system of delivery. "We Federal Expressed it back and forth," Smith, 29, explained. "I Federal Expressed the money, he Federal

Expressed the stuff. He would use a phony address for his address. I thought it was kind of creative in a way. He'd send me newspapers from Philadelphia and tape the stuff inside the papers."

During the season, he said, his supplier, who lived in Philadelphia, where Smith began his major league career, would call "and ask me if I needed anything." The supplier, Smith added, also would travel to other cities, including New York and Pittsburgh, to deliver cocaine to him.

Smith wouldn't name his supplier, but he said he identified him to F.B.I. agents who interviewed him and to the Pittsburgh grand jury when he testified. Smith was said by government officials to be one of several players who would be called to testify at the trial next month of Curtis Strong, a Philadelphia caterer who was one of seven alleged dealers indicted by the grand jury. Asked if Strong was his supplier, Smith laughed and said, "I better not say. There's more than one dealer in Philly."

Smith said marijuana had been "my drug of choice" but then "I got involved with cocaine and I started to have a problem. There's no doubt I was addicted. I started losing interest in things. I didn't care about the game. The majority of the time we were in a hurry to get the game over with and do it all over again."

"Three or four" Cardinal teammates, he said, were using cocaine with him, but "at no point did I think any of them were as hooked as I was. They had more will power to control the habit than I did."

He first used cocaine, he said, when he was playing winter baseball in 1977, before he reached the major leagues, but he said he didn't use it regularly until after the 1980 season, his first full season in the majors, "when I started making more money." The Cardinals won the World Series in 1982, and over the following winter Smith's drug use increased. "I really went over the bend with it because I didn't have anything to do," he said. "I did it almost every day during that winter."

He estimated that from 1979 until he entered rehabilitation in June 1983 for four weeks, he spent about $50,000 or $60,000 on cocaine, "give or take a few thousand. I started buying in bigger quantities, eighths and quarters. I almost tried buying an ounce." At times, he said, he used the drug with friends and teammates, but "the majority of time, you do it solo. It's so expensive and it goes so fast, you like to hoard it."

Smith acknowledged talking to players on other teams about cocaine on the field before games. "We would have conversations sometimes," he said, "trying to find out who had connections, who could get something. It was usually during practice before a game, loosening up, running sprints, talking to guys. I think that's how some of the information got around in the drug investigation."

In 1983, Smith, never considered an outstanding outfielder, played even worse than usual defensively, finishing with a .941 fielding average compared with a .970 average the year before. His success at stealing bases was also not so great as in the year before.

"I think it slowed me down, not just running but my mental thinking," Smith said, discussing the effect cocaine had on his play. "I wasn't as alert. My body was getting run-down, burnt out, as they say. I think it affected me. Other people didn't because I was still getting hits."

Smith wound up the season with a .321 batting average, 14 points better than the previous year. But over all, he said, the cocaine use affected his play.

"Look at my defense," he said. "It seemed like I was averaging two or three errors a game. I was getting picked off. Everything I swung at was away."

"Whitey thought I was having problems but not drugs," Smith said, referring to Manager Whitey Herzog. "He thought I was having emotional problems. No one wants to believe a guy is doing bad because of drug problems. But the more I did it, the worse I felt. My need kept getting greater and I couldn't fight that need."

He told of locking himself in a room, not answering the phone, not talking to anyone. "I was getting away from my family," he said. "My addiction was changing my thinking and my feelings, and I no longer was the same person."

*Using Meal Money for Purchases
on Road*

Smith's story is not different from those of others who have talked of their involvement with cocaine. The drug can become all-consuming, and the players addicted to it virtually lead their lives with it at the center. Law enforcement officials say some players would make sure their suppliers always were nearby so they wouldn't have to carry large quantities of cocaine with them. The players obtain cocaine from suppliers before games for use during the games, then make another purchase after the games for use then. They use alcohol and pills to come down from the cocaine high so they can sleep, then start with cocaine again when they wake up, again making sure the suppliers are on hand to deliver the morning's supply.

These officials also told of how some players have had their paychecks sent to their agents but still have had money to buy drugs. Among other resources, officials said, they have used the meal money they get when they are on the road and they have used money they get from shoe companies for wearing their shoes. Some players also have sold cocaine to other players as an accommodation, officials said, but there has been no indication—or at least known evidence—that any players have sold the drug for profit.

Whether or not there is evidence, clubs are careful about acquiring players who may have involvement with drugs. In fact, eyebrows around the league were raised earlier this season when the Royals obtained Smith from the Cardinals, considering the shattering experience the Royals had only two years ago.

"We checked him out thoroughly, and that's mild," Howser, the Kansas City manager, said. "A club that's been involved like we were has to be overcautious. That's the most embarrassing thing that has happened. If we're even suspicious that a guy is involved, we wouldn't go after him. I don't know that winning would be worth going through that again."

Sackful of Chicken Tips Off
a Manager

Howser was as surprised as anyone when several members of the Royals were implicated in the Kansas City drug case. He said he can look back at various incidents now and see that they might have been the result of drug use, but he said he had no way of knowing then.

"The peoples' work habits weren't as good," he said, "and when your work habits are bad, your skills decline. Their drive dropped off quite a bit. The tenacity, the ability to stay after it, they don't seem to be as tough mentally. They're kind of docile, milquetoast. The frustrating thing as a manager is you're around these guys for seven months and that slips by you."

He told of how one of the players who eventually was found to be involved walked into the clubhouse one day at 4:55 P.M. carrying a sackful of chicken. The players were supposed to be in uniform at 5 P.M.

"That's kind of a tipoff," Howser said. "The thing that disappointed me about this guy was he had good work habits; he came from a good organization. He was supposed to be in here early one day and when he didn't show up, we called him and he was asleep at 3 o'clock."

Speaking later of Willie Aikens, the first baseman who pleaded guilty to a drug charge and served time in prison, Howser said, "His work habits dropped off. He used to have a smile on his face, but his attitude changed. I thought he was mad at me or the organization."

Aikens, who hit four home runs for the Royals in the 1980 World Series, has not played well since his drug experience and this season has played in the minor leagues. He declined to talk about his cocaine use. Asked if cocaine has ended careers prematurely, Howser said, "No question about it."

The known cases of cocaine use also have made managers suspicious about other players.

"I've checked lockers and their bags while they're on the field," Billy Martin, the Yankees' manager, said, speaking of the time he managed the Oakland A's, "trying to find different stuff, people I've suspected. I've never found anything and I've tried hard."

Buck Rodgers, the Montreal manager, said he didn't have to look too hard when he managed the Milwaukee Brewers.

"One of my players came in late for a Sunday game in Minnesota," Rodgers related. "Being late was just part of it. He couldn't stop sniffing. He walked in and every player on the team watched him walk across and then everybody looked at me to see if I was watching. So everybody had some idea."

Suspicion has become a first reaction in certain instances.

"When a ballplayer shows some symptoms on the field," Jim Frey, manager of the Chicago Cubs, said, "when his personality as a player on the field changes, you question it because of today's culture. Sometimes you say to yourself, 'I wonder if maybe this fellow is using something.' That's a natural reaction."

On the other hand, Chuck Tanner, the Pittsburgh manager, whose team was the center of controversy during the drug investigation in Pittsburgh earlier this year, said he tries to resist suspicion.

"If every time a guy boots a ball, you wondered what it was, you'd go crazy," Tanner said. "Everybody makes an error. Every pitcher loses a game. Guys in the Hall of Fame lost games."

Even experience doesn't make a manager an expert, though. Rod Scurry, a Pirates relief pitcher, underwent rehabilitation for cocaine use and returned to the team. "It was up to me to take care of him after he came back," Tanner said. "So I'd ask him and he said he felt good. When he didn't show up, I was surprised. If I thought there was a problem, I would've tried to help him."

Scurry returned to rehabilitation a second time for substance abuse, though the Pirates never said the treatment was for drug abuse.

Players who have undergone treatment for cocaine use acknowledge that it is difficult to remain free of drugs afterward, not unlike an alcoholic with alcohol. Steve Howe, the relief pitcher released by Los Angeles earlier this season and recently signed by the Minnesota Twins, has been treated twice.

"You're always tempted," Lonnie Smith said. "If you socialize with people, you run across the wrong people. You're tempted almost every day out of the year. It's not easy. There's no known cure for the disease."

EDUCATING BLACK ATHLETES[4]

For decades, student athletes, usually seventeen-to-nineteen-year-old freshmen, have informally agreed to a contract with the universities they attend: athletic performance in exchange for an education. The athletes have kept their part of the bargain; the universities have not. Universities and athletic departments have gained huge gate receipts, television revenues, national visibility, donors to university programs, and more, as a result of the performances of gifted basketball and football players, of whom a disproportionate number of the most gifted and most exploited have been black.

While blacks are not the only student athletes exploited, the abuses usually happen to them first and worst. To understand why, we must understand sports' impact upon black society: how popular beliefs that blacks are innately superior athletes, and that sports are "inherently" beneficial, combine with the life circumstances of young blacks, and with the aspirations of black student athletes, to make those students especially vulnerable to victimization.

Sports at all levels are widely believed to have achieved extraordinary, if not exemplary, advances in the realm of interracial relations since the time when Jackie Robinson became the first black to play major-league baseball. To some extent, this reputation has been deliberately fostered by skilled sports propagandists eager to project "patriotic" views consistent with America's professed ideals of racial justice and equality of opportunity. To a much greater extent, however, this view of sports has been encouraged by observers of the sporting scene who have simply been naive about the dynamics of sports as an institution, about their relationship to society generally, and about the race-related realities of American sports in particular.

Many misconceptions about race and sports can be traced to developments in sports that would appear on the surface to repre-

[4]Excerpted from a magazine article by Harry Edwards, professor of sociology at the University of California at Berkeley. *Atlantic.* 252:31–8. Ag. '83. Copyright Harry Edwards 1983. Reprinted with permission.

sent significant racial progress. For instance, though blacks constitute only 11.7 percent of the U.S. population, in 1982 more than
55 percent of the players in the National Football League were
black, and, in 1981, twenty-four of the twenty-eight first-round
NFL draft choices were black. As for the two other major professional team sports, 70 percent of the players making National
Basketball Association rosters during the 1982–1983 season, and
80 percent of the starters that same season, were black, while 19
percent of America's major-league baseball players at the beginning of the 1982 season were black.

Black representation on sports honor rolls has been even more
disproportionate. For example, the past nine Heisman trophies,
awarded each year to the "best" collegiate football player in the
land, have gone to blacks. In the final rushing statistics of the 1982
NFL season, thirty-six of the top forty running backs were black.
In 1982, not a single white athlete was named to the first team
of a major Division I All-American basketball roster. Similarly,
twenty-one of the twenty-four athletes selected for the 1982 NBA
All-Star game were black. Since 1955, whites have won the
NBA's "most valuable player" award only five times, as opposed
to twenty-three times for blacks. And, of course, boxing championships in the heavier weight divisions have been dominated by
black athletes since the 1960s. But a judicious interpretation of
these and related figures points toward conclusions quite different
from what one might expect.

Patterns of opportunity for blacks in American sports, like
those in the society at large, are shaped by racial discrimination,
a phenomenon that explains the disproportionately high number
of talented black athletes in certain sports and the utter exclusion
of blacks from most other American sports, as well as from deci-
sion-making and authority positions in virtually all sports.

Most educated people today accept the idea that the level of
black representation and the quality of black performance in
sports have no demonstrable relationship to race-linked genetic
characteristics. Every study purporting to demonstrate such a relationship has exhibited critical deficiencies in methodological,
theoretical, or conceptual design. Moreover, the factors determin-
ing the caliber of sports performances are so complex and dispa-

rate as to render ludicrous any attempt to trace athletic excellence to a single biological feature.

Thus, despite a popular view that blacks are "natural" athletes, physically superior to athletes from other groups, the evidence tends to support cultural and social—rather than biological—explanations of their athletic success.

Briefly:

—Thanks to the mass media and to long-standing traditions of racial discrimination limiting blacks' access to many high-prestige occupational opportunities, the black athlete is much more visible to black youths than, say, black doctors or black lawyers. Therefore, unlike white children, who see many different potential role models in the media, black children tend to model themselves after, or to admire as symbolically masculine, the black athlete—the one prevalent and positive black success figure they are exposed to regularly, year in and year out, in America's white-dominated mass media.

—The black family and the black community tend to reward athletic achievement much more and earlier than any other activity. This also lures more young blacks into sports-career aspirations than the actual opportunities for sports success would warrant.

—Because most American sports activities are still devoid of any significant black presence, the overwhelming majority of aspiring black athletes emulate established black role models and seek careers in only four or five sports—basketball, football, baseball, boxing, and track. The brutally competitive selection process that ensues eliminates all but the most skilled black athletes by the time they reach the collegiate and advanced-amateur ranks. The competition is made all the more intense because even in these sports, some positions (such as quarterback, center, and middle linebacker in football, and catcher in baseball) are relatively closed to blacks.

—Finally, sports are seen by many black male youths as a means of proving their manhood. This tends to be extraordinarily important to blacks, because the black male in American society has been systematically cut off from mainstream routes of masculine expression, such as economic success, authority positions, and so forth.

Despite the great pool of athletic talent generated in black society, black athletes still get fewer than one in ten of the athletic scholarships given out in the United States. And, at least partially as a result of the emphasis placed upon developing their athletic talents from early childhood, an estimated 25 to 35 percent of male black high school athletes qualifying for athletic scholarships cannot accept those scholarships because of accumulated academic deficiencies. Many of these young men eventually end up in what is called, appropriately enough, the "slave trade"—a nationwide phenomenon involving independent scouts who, for a fee (usually paid by a four-year college), search out talented but academically "high-risk" black athletes and place them in accommodating junior colleges, where their athletic skills are further honed while they earn the grades they need to transfer to the sponsoring four-year schools.

Of those who are eventually awarded collegiate athletic scholarships, studies indicate, as many as 65 to 75 percent may never graduate from college. Of the 25 to 35 percent who do eventually graduate from the schools they play for, an estimated 75 percent graduate either with physical-education degrees or in majors created specifically for athletes and generally held in low repute. The problem with these "jock majors," and increasingly with the physical-education major as well, is that they make poor credentials in the job market. One might assume that ample occupational opportunities would be available to outstanding black former athletes, at least within the sports world. But the reality is quite different. To begin with, the overwhelming majority of black athletes, whether scholarship-holders or professionals, have *no* post-career occupational plans or formal preparation for any type of post-career employment either inside or outside sports. These blacks are unemployed more often, and earn less when they do have jobs, than their non-athletic college peers; they are also likely to switch jobs more often, to hold a wider variety of jobs, and to be less satisfied with the jobs they hold—primarily because the jobs tend to be dull, dead-end, or minimally rewarding.

Few Americans appreciate the extent to which the overwhelming majority of young males seeking affluence and stardom through sports are foredoomed to fail. The three major team sports provide approximately 2,663 jobs for professional athletes, regardless of color, in a nation of 226 million people, roughly half of whom are male. This means that only one American male in about 42,000 is a professional football, basketball, or baseball player.

While the proportion of blacks in professional basketball is 70 percent, in professional football 55 percent, and in professional baseball 19 percent, only about 1,400 black people (up from about 1,100 since the establishment of the United States Football League) are making a living as professional athletes in these three major sports today. And if one adds to this number all the black professional athletes in all other American sports, all the blacks in minor and semi-professional sports leagues, and all the black trainers, coaches, and doctors in professional sports, one sees that fewer than 2,400 black Americans can be said to be making a living in professional athletics today.

This situation, considered in combination with the black athlete's educational underdevelopment, helps explain why so many black athletes not only fail to achieve their expectations of life-long affluence but also frequently fall far short of the levels achieved by their non-athletic peers.

Despite the fact, then, that American basketball, boxing, football, and baseball competitions have come more and more to look like Ghana playing Nigeria, sport continues to loom like a fog-shrouded minefield for the overwhelming majority of black athletes. It has been a treadmill to oblivion rather than the escalator to wealth and glory it was believed to be. The black athlete who blindly sets out today to fill the shoes of Dr. J., Reggie J., Magic J., Kareem Abdul-J., or O.J. may well end up with "No J."—no job that he is qualified to do in our modern, technologically sophisticated society. At the end of his sports career, the black athlete is not likely to be running or flying through airports like O.J. He is much more likely to be sweeping up airports—if he has the good fortune to land even that job.

These are the tragic circumstances that prompted Joe Paterno, 1982 Division I football "Coach of the Year" of the New York Football Writers' Association, to exclaim in January from the floor of the 1983 NCAA convention in San Diego: "For fifteen years we have had a race problem. We have raped a generation and a half of young black athletes. We have taken kids and sold them on bouncing a ball and running with a football and that being able to do certain things athletically was going to be an end in itself. We cannot afford to do that to another generation." With that statement, Coach Paterno gave impetus to the passage of the NCAA's "Rule 48," which set off what is probably the most heated race-related controversy within the NCAA since the onset of widespread racial integration in major-college sports programs during the 1950s and 1960s.

Put most simply, Rule 48 stipulates that, beginning in 1986, freshman athletes who want to participate in sports in any of the nation's 227 Division I colleges and universities must have attained a minimum score of 700 (out of a possible 1,600) on the Scholastic Aptitude Test (SAT) or a score of 15 (out of a possible 36) on the American College Test (ACT), and must have achieved a C average in eleven designated high school courses, including English, mathematics, social sciences, and physical sciences. Further, as *The N.C.A.A. News* reported, Rule 48

does not interfere with the admissions policies of any Division I institution. Nonqualifiers under this legislation may be admitted and attend class. Such a student could compete as a sophomore if he or she satisfies the satisfactory-progress rules and would have four varsity seasons starting as a sophomore if he or she continues to make satisfactory progress. Further, under related Proposal No. 49-B, any student who achieves at least 2.0 in all high school courses but does not meet the new terms of No. 48 can receive athletically related financial aid in his or her first year, but cannot practice or compete in intercollegiate athletics. This student would have three varsity years of participation remaining.

The outcry in response to the passage of Rule 48 was immediate. Ironically, the most heated opposition to the rule came from black civil-rights leaders and black college presidents and educators—the very groups one might have expected to be most supportive of the action. Their concern was over those provisions of Rule 48 specifying minimum test scores as a condition for sports participation, particularly the 700 score on the SAT. Leading the black criticism of the NCAA's new academic standards were the National Association for Equal Opportunity in Higher Education (NAFEO), representing 114 traditionally black colleges and universities; the National Alliance of Black School Educators (NABSE); Rev. Jesse Jackson, president of People United to Serve Humanity (Operation PUSH); Rev. Benjamin Hooks, executive director of the National Association for the Advancement of Colored People (NAACP); and Rev. Joseph Lowery, president of the Southern Christian Leadership Conference (SCLC). They argued, first, that blacks were not consulted in the formulation of Rule 48; second, that the minimum SAT score requirement was arbitrary; and, finally, that the SAT and the ACT are racist diagnostic tests, which reflect a cultural bias favoring whites. They believed that the 700 SAT and 15 ACT score requirements would unfairly penalize black student athletes, given that 55 percent of black students generally score lower than 700 on the SAT and 69 percent score lower than 15 on the ACT. And why would the majority of NCAA Division I institutions vote to support a rule that would reduce participation opportunities for black athletes? For NAFEO and its supporters, the answer was clear. The most outspoken among the critics of Rule 48 was Dr. Jesse N. Stone, Jr., the president of the Southern University System of Louisiana, who said:

The end result of all this is the black athlete has been too good. If it Rule 48] is followed to its logical conclusion, we say to our youngsters, "let the white boy win once in a while." This has set the black athlete back twenty-five or thirty years. The message is that white schools no longer want black athletes.

Members of the American Council on Education (ACE) committee charged with developing Rule 48 vehemently denied claims that no blacks were involved in the process. Whatever the truth of the matter, the majority of black NCAA delegates felt that their interests and views had not been represented.

I could not agree more with NAFEO, Jackson, Hooks, Lowery, *et al.* on their contention that the minimum SAT and ACT test scores are arbitrary. Neither the ACE nor the NCAA has yet provided any reasoned or logical basis for setting the minimum scores. But whereas NAFEO and others say that the scores are arbitrary and too high, I contend that they are arbitrary and so *low* as to constitute virtually no standards at all. I have other, more fundamental disagreements with the NAFEO position.

One need not survey very much literature on the racist abuse of diagnostic testing in this country to appreciate the historical basis of NAFEO's concerns about rigidly applied test standards. But the demand that Rule 48 be repealed on the grounds that its test-score requirements are racist and will unfairly affect blacks is both factually contestable and strategically regrettable. The evidence is overwhelming that the SAT and the ACT discriminate principally on the basis of class, rather than race. The greater discrepancy between black and white scores occurs on the math section of the SAT, where cultural differences between the races logically would have the least impact. Even on the verbal sections of these diagnostic tests, differences in black and white scores are at least partially explained as class-related phenomena. As Dr. Mary Frances Berry, a NAFEO supporter, asserts:

A major differential among test scores] was *not* between black and white students, but between students from well-off families and students from poor families. The better-off the family, the higher the score—for whites *and* blacks.

Dr. Norman C. Francis, president of the traditionally black Xavier University of Louisiana and immediate past chairman of the College Board, agrees:

The SAT is not merely a measure of potential aptitude, as many believe, but is also an achievement test which accurately measures what students have learned to that point. Most students do poorly on the test simply because they have never been taught the concepts that will help them to understand what testing and test taking is all about. It is an educational disadvantage, not an inability to learn. . . . The plain truth is that students in poorer schools are never taught to deal with word problems and . . . critical analysis. The problem therefore is not with the students, nor with the test, but rather with an educational system which fails to teach youngsters what they need to know.

Rule 48, therefore, involves far more than a simple black-white controversy, as 1981 SAT test statistics bear out. While 49 percent of black male students in 1981 failed to achieve at least a 700 on the combined SAT, as compared with 14 percent of the whites and 27 percent of other minorities, far more whites (31,140) and other minorities (27,145) than blacks (15,330) would have been affected under Rule 48.

Furthermore, between 1981 and 1982, blacks' verbal scores rose nine points and mathematics scores rose four points, compared with a two-point gain in verbal and a one-point gain in math for the white majority.

NAFEO claims that black athletes would have less access to traditionally white Division I institutions in the wake of Rule 48. But even though proportionately more blacks score below Rule 48's minimum-score requirements, it is unlikely that significant numbers of blacks would be deprived of opportunities to attend traditionally white schools on athletic scholarships. Indeed, if the enrollment of black athletes falls off at any Division I schools for this reason, I submit that the schools most likely to suffer will be the traditionally black colleges. NCAA disciplinary records show that traditionally white institutions have led the way in amateur-athletic rules infractions and in exploiting black athletes. Why? Because they have the largest financial investment in their athletic programs, and because they and their athletic personnel stand to reap the greatest rewards from athletic success. With so much at stake, why would schools that for so long have stretched, bent, and broken rules to enroll black athletes no longer want them?

The loopholes in Rule 48 are sufficient to allow any school to recruit any athlete it really wants. Junior colleges are not covered under the rule, so schools could still secure and develop athletes not eligible for freshman sports participation at four-year Division I colleges. Further, Rule 48 allows Division I schools to recruit freshman athletes who are academically ineligible to participate, and even to provide them with financial support. After several meetings with NAFEO representatives, Rev. Jesse Jackson, and others, I am strongly convinced that for many within the ranks of Rule 48's detractors, fiscal rather than educational issues are the priority concern. The overwhelming majority of athletes recruited by traditionally black Division I schools are black, score below Rule 48 minimum-test-score requirements, and tend to need financial support in order to attend college. However, because they have far more modest athletic budgets than traditionally white schools, traditionally black schools are not nearly so able to provide financial support for both a roster of active athletes and a long roster of newly recruited athletes ineligible for athletic participation under Rule 48. Traditionally black Division I schools, already at a recruiting disadvantage owing to smaller budgets and less access to lucrative TV exposure, would be placed at an even more critical recruiting disadvantage, since they would not be able to afford even those athletes they would ordinarily be able to get.

Thus, the core issue in the Rule 48 controversy is not racist academic standards, or alleged efforts by whites to resegregate major-college sports, so much as parity between black and white institutions in the collegiate athletic arms race.

Strategically, the position of NAFEO, the NABSE, and the black civil-rights leaders vis-à-vis Rule 48 poses two problems. First, they have missed the greatest opportunity since the *Brown* v. *Board of Education of Topeka* case thirty years ago to make an impressive statement about quality and equality in education. And, since they had the attention of the nation, they also squandered a rare opportunity to direct a national dialogue on restructuring the role and stipulating the rights of athletes in the academy. Second, with no real evidence to support their claims of racist motives on the part of Rule 48's white supporters, or of simple race bias in the rule's stipulations, these black educators and civil-rights leaders left the unfortunate and unintended impression that they were against *all* academic standards because they believed that black students are unable to achieve even the moderate standards established under Rule 48.

Notwithstanding the transparent criticisms leveled by Rule 48's detractors, the measure does contain some real flaws relative to its proposed goal of shoring up the academic integrity of Division I athletic programs. First, the standards stipulated in Rule 48 are *too low.* A score of 700 on the SAT, for example, projects less than a fifty-fifty chance of graduating from most Division I schools.

Second, Rule 48 does not address in any way the educational problems of students once they have matriculated, which is where

the real educational rip-off of collegiate student athletes has occurred. Rather, it establishes standards of high school preparation
and scholastic achievement necessary for students who wish to
participate in college sports as freshmen.

Nonetheless, the NCAA action is worthy of support, not as a
satisfactory solution to the educational problems of big-time collegiate sports but as a step—a very small and perhaps even inept
step—toward dealing with these problems. Rule 48 communicates
to young athletes, beginning with those who are sophomores in
high school, that we expect them to develop academically as well
as athletically. In California, 320 students each year participate
in California Interscholastic Federation athletic programs, and
most undoubtedly aspire to win athletic scholarships to Division
I institutions. However, only 5 percent of these students will ever
participate in college sports at any level (including junior college),
and the overwhelming majority will never even enroll at a four-
year school. If Rule 48 does indeed encourage greater academic
seriousness among high school athletes, the vast majority of high
school student athletes who are *not* going on to college may benefit
most from the NCAA's action—since they face the realities of life
after sports immediately upon graduation from high school.

Further, were I not to support Rule 48, I would risk communicating to black youth in particular that I, a nationally known
black educator, do not believe that they have the capacity to
achieve a 700 score on the SAT, with three years to prepare for
the test, when they are given a total of 400 points simply for answering a single question in each of the two sections of the test,
and when they have a significant chance of scoring 460 by a purely
random marking of the test. Finally, I support the NCAA's action
because I believe that black parents, black educators, and the black
community must insist that black children be taught and that they
learn whatever subject matter is necessary to excel on diagnostic
and all other skills tests.

Outcries of "racism," and calls for black boycotts of or exemp-
tions from such tests, seem to me neither rational nor constructive
long-term responses to the problem of black students' low test
scores. Culture can be learned and taught. And this is what we
should be about as black educators—preparing our young people

to meet the challenges they face on these tests, and, by extension, in this society.

I believe that (1) student athletes and non-athletes alike should be given diagnostic tests on a recurrent basis to assure skills achievement; (2) test-score standards should and must be raised, based upon the skill demands and challenges of our contemporary world; and (3) the test standards set should be established as post-enrollment goals and not pre-enrollment obstacles.

In the case of scholarship athletes, every institution should have the right to set its own academic enrollment standards. But those same institutions *must* acknowledge a binding corollary obligation and responsibility to develop and implement support programs sufficiently effective to fulfill their implied contracts with the athletes recruited.

III. SPORTS AND VIOLENCE

EDITOR'S INTRODUCTION

To some extent, violence and sports are inseparable. Most sports require physical conflict as well as competition. The so-called blood sports, such as boxing, have violence as their *raison d'etre*; the primal appeal of boxing is the sight of one man beating another unconscious. In football, the opposing players forcefully struggle to gain territory on the field. Other team sports, such as soccer, basketball, and hockey, involve constant skirmishing for possession of the ball or puck. Even baseball, a fairly tame game by most standards, contains the possibility of fatal violence: each pitched ball is a dangerous missile that flies toward the batter at speeds as high as 100 mph. The degree of violence allowed in each sport is governed by a set of rules that levies penalties for excesses.

Is there a point at which the violent aspects of a sport, even if they are allowed by the rules, go beyond what society should permit? Some observers believe that this point is reached when there is a strong possibility that an athlete will sustain life-threatening or permanent injury. Although many sports attain this level of risk, including auto racing and polo, boxing has been singled out for the frequency with which players die or suffer serious injury in the ring. Patrick Cooke's article from *Science 84,* which opens this section, discusses brain injuries that result from head blows in boxing. Despite the evidence, however, many promoters, coaches, athletes, and fans are reluctant to tamper with the "purity" of the sport by instituting safety measures.

Violence in the arena—whether part of the game (as in boxing) or incidental to it (when fights break out between opponents) —takes on a still more dangerous dimension when it spreads to the fans. This phenomenon is analyzed in detail in the second selection, an article by Bil Gilbert and Lisa Twyman reprinted from *Sports Illustrated.* Unruly fans are in the minority at most events and are usually tolerated or ignored. But when hundreds of frenzied spectators—under the influence of alcohol, team fanaticism, or simply the contagion of the riotous impulse—turn into an uncontrollable mob, the results can be tragic. Richard Lacayo's report from *Time* magazine captures the horror of the riot at the 1985 European Soccer Cup final in Brussels that left 38 spectators crushed and suffocated to death, in the sight of 400 million viewers who were watching the game on television.

FOR WHOM THE BELL TOLLS[1]

Boxing lore has it that along the road to becoming a much-feared three-division world title holder, Roberto Duran once knocked out a horse with a single punch on a street corner in his native Panama. Knocked it out cold.

Like most professional fighters, Duran can deliver a punch with about 1,000 pounds of force. Just how much physical damage such blows can exact on the human brain has been debated since the Marquess of Queensberry sought in 1867 to civilize the men who, curiously, were to shake hands and come out fighting.

Between 1945 and 1982, the "sweet science" killed 349 of them. Eleven have died in the last two years. One victim was Duk Koo Kim, an obscure lightweight who suddenly found himself in line for the big money in 1982. In the 13th round of a contest with Ray "Boom Boom" Mancini at Caesar's Palace, the exhausted Kim took more than 40 punches and then in the 14th received the final shocking blow that sent him sliding to the canvas. Despite emergency surgery, his brain never again showed electrical activity, and he was declared dead.

According to Ira Casson, a neurologist at Long Island Jewish–Hillside Medical Center, that last blow was responsible for Kim's death: "It was one hell of a punch." Not only is it force, says Casson, but placement that makes for a killer-punch. "A shot to the temple or the point of the chin are the ones that do the most

[1]Reprint of a magazine article by journalist Patrick Cooke. *Science 84.* 5:88–9. D. '84. Reprinted by permission of Science 84 Magazine. © 1984 by the American Association for the Advancement of Science.

damage," he says. Because the head more easily moves side to side than front to back, blows that twist the head or tilt it sideways produce the quickest, most violent movement of the head.

It is the rapidity of the head's movement that most often causes brain damage—and death. The human brain is suspended in fluid inside the skull. When hit hard, the skull twists and the brain, like a subway rider caught off-guard by a lurching train, whirls and slams against the sides of its hard skeletal casing. Nerve tissue can be bruised, and blood vessels along the surface of the brain can tear and bleed.

If jolted hard enough, tissue from deep inside the brain begins to bleed as well. Because the skull is unyielding, pressure quickly crushes the brain against the hard surface intended to protect it. Nerve cells begin to die and the brain stem, control center for vital functions like breathing and heartbeat, is squeezed off from oxygen.

Olympic coach Emanuel Steward, whose Kronk Gym in Detroit has produced such champions as Thomas "Hit Man" Herns and Milt McCrory, says that instinct and conditioning save many boxers from the devastating blow. They learn to literally roll with the punches. "You look at somebody like Ali," he says. "It may have appeared as though he was getting hit hard, but he knew how to move with a punch to soften it."

The big problem, says Steward, is that fights are just too long. As a fighter tires in the 13th, 14th, and 15th rounds of a bout, his reflexes become slower and neck muscles become less effective at buffering a powerful punch. "When your body is drained, it's easier to make mistakes. And that's when you get hurt."

Equally as tragic as the man killed in the ring are the legions of fighters who retire after years of taking toe-to-toe punches out of the painful belief that, with just a few more bouts, they could have been contenders. "There's a whole spectrum of brain damage," says Casson, "that goes from the staggering punch-drunk guy you can spot at 30 yards right down to the fighter whose problems only show up on neurological tests."

According to Casson, more than half of professional boxers will eventually be bested by chronic brain damage. In addition to electronic tests such as the electroencephalogram (EEG)—which monitors electrical activity of the brain—and sophisticated X rays like the CAT-scan, Casson recently gave a group of active and retired boxers neuropsychological exams. The tests measured the boxers' accuracy recalling simple designs and sentences, connecting dots, and drawing geometric figures. Every boxer showed at least one abnormal sign. What's more, he says, the tests paralleled abnormalities that appeared in the boxers' EEG and CAT-scans.

There is no area of a typical professional boxer's brain that escapes at least some injury. The outermost layer, for example, can wear down from repeatedly chafing against the skull. Since this area controls speech, memory, and complex thinking, damage to it can cause slurring, forgetfulness, and mood shifts.

The most pronounced damage occurs in the brain's interior, where spinal fluid is stored in hollow spaces called ventricles. As punches shake the skull, tissue around the spaces atrophies, enlarging the ventricles. In severe cases a canal opens up between them. This area of the brain is thought to control the coordination and balance that allows ballet dancers and prizefighters alike to remain on their feet. Once it is impaired, tremors similar to those seen in Parkinson's disease can occur, as well as the unsteady gait that marks the punch-drunk.

Coach Steward maintains that while the fighter's trade is no tea dance, the image of the dizzy has-been is much exaggerated. Traditionally, the boxers thought to be most often injured were the "sluggers"—usually heavyweights—and not the artful dodgers. Steward insists that in his 32 years in the profession he's seen only a few men he thought had problems—which, he argues, they may have had before they started in the ring. "Take somebody like Jake LaMotta or Archie Moore," he says. "LaMotta was a slugger and had over 100 fights. They're both very intelligent, articulate men today."

But even the man who could float like a butterfly appears to have been stung by a long career in the ring. Muhammad Ali recently underwent diagnostic tests to determine the cause of his sometimes-slurred speech and hand tremors. His doctors said he is suffering from a collection of symptoms loosely called Parkinson's syndrome, similar to Parkinson's disease but much milder. They did not say that boxing was the cause of the syndrome.

But others think that Ali's condition was all but inevitable. "They're using semantics to whitewash his condition," says Casson. "I'm not 100 percent sure, but it all fits into the pattern of problems typically suffered by boxers. After all, how many 42-year-olds have Parkinson's disease?"

Although Casson would agree that being punch-drunk may not be mentally debilitating—several of his test subjects are now successful businessmen—he cautions that later in life real problems might arise. "Some say it's progressive, some say it stops if you stop fighting—maybe gets a little better. Nobody knows. But everyone over 25 is losing brain cells every day. People who've had injuries like these boxers lose their reserve capacity of cells. When they get older, they won't be able to cover it up."

Nearly everybody agrees that there is room for greater safety measures. Besides reducing the number of rounds in a bout, researchers also recommend shorter rounds, more padding in boxing gloves, less emphasis on head blows in scoring, and a mandatory helmet rule. Others say that there should be a fixed retirement age for boxers and a limit to the number of fights in a career. "The syndrome is definitely related to the number of bouts," says Casson. "A boxer who starts at age 25 is going to last longer than one who starts at 15."

But because boxing is regulated on a state-by-state basis, these changes may be slow in coming. "In Communist countries things are easier," says Casson. "They just say 'Okay everybody, HEAD-GEAR!' and suddenly they're all wearing it. Things aren't that simple here."

These measures are unlikely to satisfy the American Medical Association, however, which has called for a ban on the sport for the second time in as many years. In a recent editorial the *Journal of the American Medical Association* called boxing fans bloodthirsty, promoters greedy, and said that ringside doctors are pressured to keep the "carnage" going.

Boxing is so firmly ingrained in the American scene, however, a ban could simply drive the sport to a less visible—and more dangerous—underground existence. But in any incarnation boxing's threat to boxers will not disappear.

"People love a good fight," says Casson, an admitted boxing fan. "But there are always going to be injuries and death when people get hit in the head. Some of these new measures will eliminate some of that but not all. Not when these guys hit that hard. Not when one punch can do it."

VIOLENCE: OUT OF HAND IN THE STANDS[2]

Perhaps because we're so heavily bombarded with dire news and doomsday prophecies, there's a temptation for those concerned with a problem—whether it be viral skin disorders, reading deficiencies of youth or the drying up of swamps—to call attention to it by stridently suggesting that if it isn't immediately solved the Republic will crumble. This is an especially suspect and ludicrous practice when applied to sports. The difficulties of junky jocks, sneaky coaches or greedy promoters are seldom related in any significant way to the substantial ills of society. This should be kept in mind as we consider the subject of this report, fan violence.

Through the ages sporting spectators have been notorious for hooliganism. The original Olympics were suspended because of belligerent crowd behavior. In one three-day period in 532 A.D., during the reign of the Emperor Justinian, 30,000 Romans died in riots at the chariot races. In year 1314 Edward II of England banned "that dreadful game, football," because it touched off such bloody brawls among 14th-century fans. The worst recent outburst of this sort occurred in Lima, Peru, where at a soccer match in 1964, 300 people were killed and 500 injured. There have always been incidents of this kind, but their number and seriousness fluctuate, reflecting, some theorize, disorders in the real world. (The hypothesis that behavior at sports events may serve as a barometer for measuring pressures and tension in society is probably the most thought-provoking aspect of this phenomenon.)

[2]Reprint of a magazine article by journalists Bil Gilbert and Lisa Twyman. Reprinted courtesy of *Sports Illustrated* (58:62+.) from the January 31, 1983 issue. Copyright © 1983 Time Inc. All rights reserved.

Currently, nearly all knowledgeable sources think there is a rising level of fan violence in the U.S. The consensus is that, in comparison to 20 or even 10 years ago, it's more difficult and expensive to control sports crowds; that they cause more personal injury and property damage and are uglier in manner and mood. Now, this is bad news for sport, but it hardly constitutes a grave threat to public order, health and morals. In any general discussion of violence, that which occurs at sports events is little more than an aside. During the past year, on any number of days in the Middle East or Central America there was more violence than has occurred in all of modern sports history. Spending an evening at Yankee Stadium now may be more risky than going to the zoo or staying at home, but it's still safer than walking for three hours in the neighborhood around Yankee Stadium. What fan violence amounts to may be suggested by the following sampler of happenings in recent years:

• After the WBC California State Junior Lightweight Boxing Championship in Sacramento last summer, a brawl broke out and eventually involved, police estimated, 75 to 100 fans. Before it was over, seven spectators had been stabbed, four requiring hospitalization.

• At a Friday night of boxing in Madison Square Garden in 1978, two men were stabbed, another man was shot (by an off-duty corrections officer) and a woman was treated for a severe head laceration after being struck by a bottle. While the police were carrying the gunshot victim from the Garden, someone lobbed an exploding cherry bomb at them.

• At New York's Shea Stadium during a 1978 Jets-Steelers game, spectators overpowered a security guard and dropped him over a railing to a concrete walkway 15 feet below. He suffered a fractured skull, along with a concussion and various neck injuries.

• At a 1981 Rams-Bears game in Chicago's Soldier Field there were 31 arrests, the principal charges being battery, disorderly conduct and possession of drugs. Two security men and several ushers were attacked by fans, one of whom dropped his pants and shot a moon for the benefit of the Honey Bears, the Chicago cheerleaders, and the ABC television cameras.

• In 1980 the Detroit Tigers temporarily closed the bleacher section in their stadium to retake it, so to speak, from chronically violent spectators. For the same reason, in May, 1981 the Cincinnati Reds asked their players and the opposing players, the Pittsburgh Pirates, to leave the field at Riverfront Stadium until the rowdy crowd could be brought under control.

• During a 1981 American League playoff game at Yankee Stadium, a fan carrying a blackjack ran onto the field and charged and knocked down the third-base umpire, who was saved from injury by the quick intervention of the Yankees' Graig Nettles and Dave Winfield.

• Pittsburgh Outfielder Dave Parker claims to be the No. 1 target of fan violence in America because he is black, highly paid, hasn't performed well the last couple of seasons and is proud, perhaps even a bit arrogant. He has been pelted with apple cores, hundreds of paper beer cups, jawbreakers, transistor-radio batteries and bullets (thrown not fired), as well as obscenities and racial slurs. "You ain't nothin' but a stinkin', lousy nigger" is a printable example of the latter. Once, in his hotel room in Philadelphia, Parker received a telephone call from a man who informed him that if he came down to the lobby he would be killed. Parker did and wasn't. He's among the growing number of sports figures who have received death threats during the past five years.

The list of such happenings isn't endless, but it's very long. Beyond those that draw public attention there are innumerable violent acts that go unreported. It's fair to say that on game day in every major sporting facility there are a few fights and several minor assaults and a dozen or so spectators are ejected because of bad conduct.

"This crowd violence thing has been in the dark for so long," says David M. Schaffer, director of park operations (including security) for the Chicago White Sox, a team that recently has made notable efforts to face up to its problems. "Hell, just go anywhere and there will be a fight of one kind or another."

Traditionally, the sporting establishment has been mum on the subject, believing that a certain amount of crowd misbehavior is part of the game and one which, like the legs of a Victorian lady, gentlemen speak of euphemistically; that talking about violence would focus attention on it and stimulate others to commit it; that the subject is bad for business. "We prefer to talk about crowd involvement rather than violence," said a Philadelphia Flyers official several years ago. "Violence has such an ugly connotation."

However, the fact that buying a ticket to a game markedly increases a customer's chances of getting a punch in the snoot, doused with beer, an earful of X-rated language or a vandalized car makes it difficult to sustain former traditions and illusions. By their actions, if not their words, most sports executives indicate that they regard fan violence as a large problem, one that's going to get larger, more expensive and more embarrassing if something isn't done about it soon. As never before, leagues and teams are trying to find out why their fans have grown so difficult to handle, and in making such assessments, sports executives are calling in "violence experts," a new breed of consultant.

Some of the observations, theories and conclusions of these violence experts are:

• Sports crowds generally follow some vague rules of order—for example, people don't usually stand and block the view of other spectators—but can become unstable, erratic and edgy human organizations. Within a crowd there are many low-level sources of tension—close, involuntary contact with strangers, abnormal physical discomforts, competition for territory, goods, services and information—that frustrate individuals and make them more irritable and belligerent than they are when alone or in smaller groups. Crowds provide anonymity and encourage miscreants to act more irresponsibly than they might in situations where they can be easily identified and punished. Simple, primitive emotions, such as elation, anger, panic and vengeance, are contagious within a crowd and create so-called mass hysteria. Sports events regularly draw the largest crowds of any public events, but sports facilities, compared to those offered to other crowds, are often among the most inefficient, uncomfortable and unattractive. If the environment were as grim and aggravating at art galleries, lecture halls and movie theaters as it is at Schaefer Stadium, there probably would be more disturbances at those places.

• Sports events are exhibitions of skill, grace, strength, coordination and other attractive human properties. They're also contrived, dramatic charades, of which violence is an intrinsic element or, at least, violence is not too far below the surface. In some sports, such as boxing, football and hockey, the scripts are explicitly violent. Even in those sports where the participants are not called upon to push, shove and beat each other the action is confrontational, with one individual or team trying to demolish, as the scribes say, an opponent—or crush, roll over, thump, trample, pulverize, stick it to and kill him, as they also say. The underlying themes of competitive games are strikingly similar to those of war, and the language of the two activities has become almost identical.

Our newspapers, magazines, books, TV shows, movies, theater, music and advertisements testify to our fascination with violence, that it rates not far behind sex in its vicarious attraction. One explanation for this is that many people would like to be more violent than they are. They find the idea of taking arms against their enemies—or people who merely frustrate or cause them trouble—and flattening them, so to speak, by direct physical action to be very appealing. Most people don't act on such impulses because of the law, ethics or the fear of getting hurt. Stymied by reality, they take deep satisfaction in watching and identifying with others who seem to be acting in this bold way. As a group, athletes are encouraged and rewarded for being violent while onstage, and sport has become one of our most successful devices for providing fantasy relief.

Sports crowds are encouraged to respond freely to the action of the game. Cheering, booing, hissing, stamping feet, waving fists and screaming criticisms and threats are considered normal at games, though those activities would be treated as aberrant and unruly in other circumstances. As tragedies can bring their audiences to tears and comedies can provoke laughter, sport can make its crowds a bit more violent. And as in other forms of show business, the assumption is that the more powerful the production the more pronounced the reaction of the audience.

Michael Smith, a former football and hockey player and hockey coach, is a Canadian sociologist interested in such matters. He says, "I believe that violence in sport contributes to violence in the crowd, as opposed to the notion of catharsis, that viewing violent acts results in draining away feelings of violence. I have looked at newspaper accounts of 68 episodes of collective violence or riots among spectators during or after sporting events, and in three-quarters of those the precipitating event was violence in the game. Yet for decades and decades eminent scholars wrote without a shred of evidence that acts of violence in sport are cathartic or therapeutic for spectators." Indeed, the catharsis theory is still advanced occasionally but, as Smith suggests, has been largely discredited by social scientists simply because nobody can find cases where this saltpeter-like effect has been produced.

The association between sport and violence isn't aberrant. However, it's supposedly understood by everyone involved that what's going on is just a game, a staged conflict. That this is frequently forgotten is testimony to the power of sports. Even participants who have long rehearsals and the rules of the game and referees to remind them that they are actors in a play get carried away by the make-believe battle. Losing one's grip on reality happens more often in the stands. Spectators have few restraints on their behavior, and it isn't surprising that some of them give vent to their own fantasies by responding physically to the fictitious battle being played out by the athletes. "The crowd is going crazy" is an instructive sporting cliché.

Dr. John Cheffers, a former Australian football player and international track athlete and coach, is a professor of education at Boston University. For a decade he has been professionally interested in fan violence and now offers his services to sports organizations, among them the New England Patriots. For some time Cheffers and an associate, a sociologist named Dr. Jay Meehan, have been using video equipment and graduate students to observe spectators at football, hockey, soccer and baseball games in order to identify types and causes of what they call "incongruous behavior."

Cheffers and Meehan have been investigating whether "unwarranted" actions by athletes, *i.e.*, fights, elicit exceptional responses from fans. Here their findings have been surprising. In soccer, fights among the players have triggered violence in the stands in 57% of the cases the researchers have observed. For football and baseball the percentages are 49 and 34, respectively. However, in hockey only 8.5% of the on-ice fights touched off acts of fan violence. Cheffers speculates that hockey customers see so many fights that they have become a bit blasé about them. He suggests that hockey may be moving in the direction of what he calls the "giggle sports," professional wrestling and Roller Derby. At these attractions, ostensibly illegal and violent acts by the participants are so common and highly stylized that they are largely regarded as phony and have lost much of their impact.

Such information as Cheffers and a few others have collected tends to confirm the commonsense observation that the rougher the game the rougher the crowd. Cheffers believes that "If it (violence) is on the field it will be in the stands." Contact sports provide most of the examples of fan violence, while in golf, tennis and track they are rare. But if this is the rule, there are many exceptions and anomalies. Outside the U.S., soccer, not a contact sport, has the most dangerous and destructive fans. This may be because of social and economic factors. There's a strong tradition in Europe, and particularly in the British Isles, that soccer is a workingman's game, and the rowdyism of the spectators may be, Cheffers speculates, a kind of class statement, a means of showing contempt for polite society and cocking a snoot at the well-behaved gentry.

Boxing is the most violent of all sports, but its crowds are not exceptionally disorderly. However, when something does stir them, they often become more vicious than other fans. In the U.S. during the past 10 years, *all* of the disturbances in which spectators have had at each other with knives and guns, with the intent to kill and maim, have occurred in boxing crowds. Apparently, the nature of the sport enables its fans to deal sanely with a lot of violence, but when they lose control, it's with great ferocity. Baseball may demonstrate the opposite side of the hockey-boxing coin. Small, fairly tame acts of violence on a baseball field may appear to be much worse than they really are because the game generally lacks physical contact. Also at the heart of baseball is one of the most explicitly warlike charades in all sport: the repeated and possibly fatal confrontation between pitcher and batter.

In many cases the players' unwarranted (illegal, according to the rules) acts, which Cheffers finds are likely to stir up fans, are unintentional or accidental. When an athlete makes mistakes in judgment—say, commits a dumb foul—he sometimes becomes so aroused that he begins fighting or throwing a tantrum. In other cases such displays are a matter of design and are performed for inspirational reasons or in the hope of achieving competitive advantage. Baiting umpires is a traditional baseball tactic that also incites spectators, whose calls of kill the ump or throw the bum out are often followed by fisticuffs in the stands and objects thrown out of them. Jack Dunn III, the vice-president for stadium operations of the Baltimore Orioles, says that the most fights he ever saw in the stands occurred on a day when former Oriole Manager Earl Weaver argued with an umpire and was ejected from the game. Last summer Sam Rutigliano, coach of the Cleveland Browns, in effect came down on the side of unnecessary roughness in the NFL. He said that while officials might still penalize his players for such infractions of league rules, he wasn't going to reinforce the refs' authority by fining, as he had the year before, Browns who drew unnecessary roughness calls. He said that he thought worrying about being assessed such fines might interfere with the concentration of his players and lower their morale.

Perhaps more regularly than any other sporting figures, basketball coaches attempt to incite and exploit crowd reaction by means of histrionic displays. "There's no question about it," says Shelby Metcalf, the basketball coach at Texas A&M. "Some coaches—we have a couple here in the Southwest Conference—try to get their home crowds fired up and use them to intimidate opposing players and officials. I think it works less often than these coaches and the press think it does because the players and officials are more sophisticated than they used to be. But it works often enough that there are coaches who continue to use the technique to try to get an edge. It is a danger and a disgrace to the game. We ought to be doing more than we are to stop it."

Metcalf is an unusual and unusually well-qualified authority on fan violence. In addition to having coached the Aggies for 19 seasons, he has a Ph.D. from A&M in philosophy. For his doctoral dissertation on crowd behavior and control, Metcalf selected 84 variables, ranging from the deportment of cheerleaders to the size of arena, that he thought might influence crowd actions. His list was sent to the Southwest Conference office. After each of the 112 basketball games used in the survey, referees, coaches and sports information directors on the scene were asked to check the factors that seemed to have most influenced the fans. Tabulating the results, Metcalf found, again to the surprise of no one, that the behavior of coaches, players and officials had the most effect, good and bad, on the spectators. Commenting tangentially, Metcalf says, "It's sad but true. If there's a good fight, one that gets a lot of attention in the press, attendance is going to be up for two or three weeks afterward for games of the teams involved."

Though sports entrepreneurs may not deliberately set out to pump up their customers to the point of belting each other or trashing stadiums, many team officials are inclined to stimulate frenzy and emphasize the wilder aspects of the entertainment being offered. Touting mayhem has been the principal promotional thrust of wrestling and Roller Derby. There are chronic suspicions that hockey moguls, despite repeated pious protests to the contrary, are inclined to regard brawls as good for business. The late and unlamented professional box-lacrosse league advertised itself as putting on happenings that Attila the Hun and anybody with a taste for blood and battle would love.

There are a good many sporting hypes—provocative cheerleaders, drums, horns, organs, posters, cartoons, effigy burnings, pep rallies, exploding and smart-aleck scoreboards—that have become so common that nobody thinks much about their subliminal messages and influence anymore. For example, like many other major league baseball teams, the Baltimore Orioles have an official mascot, in this case a guy in bird drag who hops around Memorial Stadium to entertain and exhort the home crowd. Among other stunts of the Baltimore bird: Between innings he dons boxing gloves and goes a few rounds with someone dressed to represent the opponents, say the Detroit Tigers, before scoring a KO, to the delight of the fans.

Pat Sullivan's family operates the Patriots, and he's the club officer concerned with crowd control. Having listened to various theories about why spectators are so unruly, Sullivan says in effect that while the ideas are interesting, "the main thing is so many of the fans are drunk."

Many other sports officials have made the same observation. Buffalo's Don Guenther, the manager of Rich Stadium, home of the Bills, says he thinks 99% of the arrests at games are related to alcohol.

Dick Vertlieb now is an entertainment and financial consultant in Seattle but in the past has been the general manager of three NBA teams, the Warriors, Pacers and Sonics, and of baseball's Seattle Mariners. "The problem," says Vertlieb, speaking of fan violence, is the "goddamn beer. All the teams do is push beer and push beer, and then when someone gets out of line, they send the cops after the guy. When I was with the Sonics there was no beer in the Coliseum and it was a family event. Now it's difficult even to take your wife. It's an outrage."

The connection between guzzling and fan violence needs very little explanation. Nobody has ever suggested that a good way to calm down a crowd is to fill it to the gills with strong drink. To a greater degree than at any other assemblies, except perhaps stag conventions, alcohol is made available to sports spectators, and they are encouraged to use it freely. There are 63 stadiums and arenas in the U.S. that serve major pro teams. Beer is sold in 61 of them and hard liquor in 24. (Only a handful of colleges sell beer at their games. This is almost universally accepted as a principal reason why collegiate crowds, despite their youth and exuberance, present fewer serious security problems than do professional ones.)

Why beer and booze, despite being named by many executives as a main cause of fan violence, are so readily available is also fairly obvious. They are profitable. How profitable can't be precisely determined, because teams and concessionaires don't routinely divulge sales figures. However, it seems likely that where beer is sold it accounts for about half of the overall concession take. This would work out to about $500,000 a season generated by a team such as the Sonics.

Beyond the retail income, the alcohol business is profitable for sports organizations in many other ways. Radio and TV broadcasts of virtually every major league game are sponsored in whole or part by breweries. According to a 1982 survey conducted by Simmons Market Research Bureau, the heavy beer-drinker is a sports lover. Male heavy beer-drinkers represent 30% of the total beer-drinking public and are responsible for nearly 80% of the total volume of beer sales.

The relationship of beer and booze to sports is so profitable that managerial types are loath to finger in-park sales as a contributing cause of fan violence. Invariably, they say the real problem is with contraband stuff, *i.e.*, alcohol that's brought to the ball park by fans in coolers, brown bags or their bloodstreams.

Joe McDermott, the Boston Red Sox executive in charge of security at Fenway Park, says that most of the Sox spectator trouble occurs in the first few innings of a game and is caused by people who were soused on arrival. "Let's face it," says McDermott, his righteous instincts overcoming his commercial caution, "it's pretty hard to get loaded on the beer sold here—it's mostly froth." Like many other teams, the Red Sox have and exercise the right to search incoming customers, confiscate containers and refuse entry to those who seem likely to make trouble.

Though, again, it's not much talked about for obvious reasons, spectator use of drugs, notably marijuana, cocaine and Quaaludes, seems to be increasing more rapidly than alcohol consumption. "Get yourself a Coke with whatever you smoke," chants a Schaefer Stadium soft-drink vendor. "Get your hot pretzels, ludes and joints," responds a mocking fan. In many arenas particular ramps and rest rooms are favored by the heads and dealers. The dangers and morality of drug use can be debated elsewhere, but there's no reason to believe that numbers of people with rolling eyeballs or runny noses make a constructive contribution to the good behavior of sports crowds.

To improve crowd control in 1976, the Red Sox began employing 20 football players from local colleges. During games they roam Fenway with the aim of soothing potentially troublesome fans or unobtrusively giving the heave-ho to those—sometimes 30 a game—who are beyond pacifying. Sox management has been pleased with the footballers, whose size gives them respect as well as clout and whose youth gives them rapport with the sort of spectators most likely to be difficult. Security people everywhere single out 20-to-30-year-old males as the most likely to create disturbances. The general opinion is that they are especially vulnerable to macho fantasies and to acting them out when stirred up by sporting events.

Wayne Thornton, 6´3´´, 230-pound Holy Cross graduate, was a member of the Fenway patrol last summer and says of his routine activities, "We look for drunks, of course, and very loud belligerent types. Every couple of innings we check out some of the rest rooms and ramps for people smoking and snorting dope. Also, we watch for guys who aren't paying much attention to the game, just waiting around and hanging out."

It's perhaps arbitrary to say that hangers-out come to an event with the intention of being violent. But there's reason to believe that the possibility of bashing heads is on their minds and an attraction in itself. Dr. Arnold R. Beisser, a Los Angeles psychiatrist with an interest in sports, has commented, "We're seeing a new use of violence. It's being used not as a means to an end but for recreational purposes, for pleasure. It's an end in itself."

A 24-year-old man—let's call him Tim—is a hanger-out type. (He won't be better identified because there's a suspicion that he might regard any public mention as a feather in his cap, a glorification of his deeds.) Tim has a better than average blue-collar job and a decent apartment in the suburbs of a Midwestern metropolis that supports franchises in all major professional sports. He has no dependents, only temporary girl friends and, therefore, a considerable amount of disposable income. Even so, he says that he doesn't regard his life as being all that good. As to ambitions? "I don't know," he says. "Livin', I guess. I got a lot of things I want to do: One, get rich. How? I don't know. I wish I knew."

Tim is a wispy 5´6´´ and weighs 120 or so pounds. But there's an indefinable quality about him—insolence, sullenness, rebelliousness—that suggests he could be trouble. "Tim," says an acquaintance, "is the kind of person that a cop will pick out of a crowd when there's a disturbance, or somebody will come up to and slug for no real reason. Maybe he looks like a loser."

Tim wasn't a high school athlete and isn't a rabid sports fan in the sense of being particularly knowledgeable or attached to a given team. However, he goes to a number of events to pass his time. At the moment, his favorite sport is hydroplane racing. He will drive long distances to attend regattas with groups of friends. "We'll get a hotel or room someplace," he says. "No showers. You know. Usually girls go, just to have fun, wherever there is a race. It's just mostly, I don't know, they just look so excellent in the water, all the spray and everything."

Last April, Tim and a dozen or so male cronies went to a hockey playoff game. Some of the gang allegedly had been to a baseball game earlier in the afternoon and had amused themselves and provoked security men by throwing snowballs at the players on the field. Tim wasn't with them and wasn't, he says, drunk before leaving for the hockey game. "I'm not saying I haven't gone like that to the races and stuff," he says. "I'll drink and stuff, but I don't get obliviated [*sic*] where it's not going to be worth it to me if I can't know what's going on when I leave."

Tim said he had a couple of beers before arriving and only one at the game. His version of what went on there is as follows. He says that toward the end of the game some trouble started in the section where he was sitting; he thinks maybe people started pouring beer on each other after a fight broke out on the ice. He and his friends edged into the melee to see the action. Then, he says, spectators and cops started grabbing people. The next thing he knew he woke up in a hospital with five broken teeth. According to security men on the scene and police records, Tim and his pals were the instigators of the brawl, dumping beer on people, threatening those around them and throwing whatever was at hand on the ice. (The players on the ice actually stopped skating to watch the fight in the stands, but not before one player tripped over some of the debris, separated his shoulder and was sidelined for the rest of the playoffs.) Tim himself imprudently attacked a very large, bearded customer, who was the one who cold-cocked him, literally driving his teeth down his throat. Tim was arrested, and pleaded guilty to charges of assault and battery and mob action. He was fined and barred by the stadium management from attending any games there for a year. Nevertheless, he thinks that the whole thing was a mistake, that he got a bum rap. He pleaded guilty, he says, only because he didn't know what really happened. "I know what I am, and that ain't it," he says. "You know what was said? It was all turned around so I came out being troublemaker

Tim, you know, and that ain't true, but that's me against the world. Whoever believes it and whoever don't."

"I believe the incidences of violence are way up," says Dr. Irving Goldaber, a sociologist who is the director and founder of the Center for Study of Crowd and Spectator Behavior, a Miami-based research and consulting firm. "My file of current incidents gets larger and larger every year. Where about 10 years ago I had one folder, now every year I do another file drawer."

Goldaber, who has advised the NFL, major league baseball and the International Association of Chiefs of Police, among others, is perhaps the country's best-known expert on fan violence. He says that five years ago he was receiving about three requests a year to appear as an expert witness in court actions having to do with incidents involving sporting crowds. Now he's getting about one every two weeks.

During the 1950s and '60s, Goldaber, who says, "Human conflict was always my field," instructed law-enforcement groups in dealing with street disturbances, protesters, terrorists and hostage takers. In the mid '70s, he says, he detected the emergence of a new form of violence in this country. He terms it "violence for vicarious power" and finds it's most openly manifested in sporting crowds, whose behavior is now one of his principal professional interests. Like many other experts Goldaber believes that the problems of sport reflect larger ones in society. Specifically, he says, "More and more people aren't making it. You work hard, you exist, but you haven't got much to show for it. There are increasing numbers of people who are deeply frustrated because they feel they have very little power over their lives. They come to sporting events to experience, vicariously, a sense of power."

In a stadium, the power trippers are even more vulnerable to ordinary crowd stimuli and irritations than more traditional fans. "They respond to the violence on the field," says Goldaber. "They respond to the hype and hoopla of the event, to the beer, cheerleaders, scoreboards and bands. When you have a crowd that is anticipating a physical experience, it will have a physical experience."

Goldaber believes that several characteristics distinguish the vicarious power-seekers. They're very prone to overidentify with a team or individuals. "They're dressed in the numbers and the letters and the names and the colors, with the jackets, the sweaters, the scarves and the pennants," he says. "They're part of the team and they're in the game." They aren't particularly concerned or knowledgeable about how games are played and take little pleasure in stylish athletic performances. "The reason they come to sporting events isn't so much to watch the game as to be in the game and especially to experience winning through their team or hero. In this world, where so many individuals are diminished, it's pretty important to matter, to win, to be No. 1. When their team wins, they have a sense of being important: 'I won.'

"Because they overidentify and think they're in the game, they feel they have a right to affect the outcome of the game, in the old ways by cheering and booing, but also with new violent forms of threatening and intimidating action. Because winning, being No. 1, is everything, they're likely to be very ferocious if they—their team—are thwarted and they vent their frustrations physically against players, officials or other spectators. That's the nub of the problem."

Goldaber feels that a vicious cycle has been created. Sensing the obsessive mood, sports management has tended to pander to it, overpromoting fan identification. Goldaber has developed this theme perhaps more fully than others, but that there's a connection between fan violence and win-at-all-cost attitudes has occurred to many. Lennie Wirtz, a veteran basketball referee who has had visions of an enraged spectator coming at him with an ice pick, says he thinks the most important reason for the worsening of behavior of coaches and players—and because of them, crowds—is the enormous pressure to win that's now at work on the participants.

Bill Veeck, a shrewd and iconoclastic baseball entrepreneur and observer for more than half a century, agrees with Wirtz. "Unfortunately, like Dr. Frankenstein, people in baseball have created a monster," Veeck says. "They think only a winning club is any good. People forget that we're in the entertainment business. Look what you get then, a George Steinbrenner. What more horrible fate could possibly happen, unless you get two?"

Many authorities say there's evidence that things could get worse. Based on information provided by police departments from around the nation, Goldaber makes the ominous estimate that in any large pro sports crowd somewhere between 0.5% and 2% of the spectators are now carrying concealed weapons. This works out to 250 to 1,000 fans packing guns, lethal knives or Wirtz's ice pick in a crowd of 50,000. Goldaber believes it's likely that we will shortly have a sports assassination, carried out by a demented fan who will rise up with, say, a 30-30 and take out a quarterback or power forward. "And when it happens once," he says, "there will be enormous publicity and this will trigger more of it. Years ago, if somebody said that we would have weapons checks before boarding airplanes it would have been thought absurd, but that's normal now and may well become normal at sporting events. Hostage-seizing at games is also a possibility. In a sense, we have already had it. Death threats are really hostage situations in which an athlete is told not to play in a certain way or be killed."

Neither Goldaber's facts nor predictions much surprise other crowd-control professionals. As to the 30-30 scenario, Cheffers remarks, "Actually, it's surprising it hasn't happened. In this country athletes are at least as celebrated as rock stars or politicians. There are a lot of Hinckleys out there who have strong feelings about sport."

Cheffers finds it easy to imagine that because of such a disaster, or in an attempt to prevent one, high-security measures might alter sport as drastically as the violence itself. "We could reach a point where major sporting events are staged in shielded areas before 5,000 or so spectators who pay several hundred dollars each for safe, luxurious accommodations," Cheffers says. "Attending live sporting events could disappear as a popular entertainment."

All of this is prophesy, but events that have occurred suggest that such possibilities should be taken seriously. The almost reflexive response of sports promoters to bad crowd situations is to lay on more cops of one sort or another. Following an ugly Monday-night football game, Sullivan said that to prevent further outbursts he would "bring in the National Guard if we have to to make things safe." Attack dogs were used for crowd control in a 1980 World Series game in Philadelphia and in 1982 in St. Louis.

This prompted Goldaber to quip, "If dogs aren't effective [he thinks they are], maybe they'll bring out attack lions next." Both the Patriots and Red Sox are converting sections of their stands into posh, heavily guarded apartment-like boxes that lease for $20,000 to $36,000 a year. Most other stadiums have, or are planning, similar facilities. Elsewhere, the ultimate crowd-control technique has already been employed. Because of reasonable fears about the conduct of supporters of rival teams, soccer games in England and American high school football and basketball games have been played in facilities from which all fans have been barred.

If we evolve into a Brave New World society, we'll no doubt have Rollerball games and Orwellian crowds—or none of either—because sport cannot be maintained in splendid isolation. Furthermore, given the nature of crowds and sport, there are probably no steps that can, or should, be taken to make spectators as pacific as Quakers at meeting. However, with these basic reservations, students of crowd behavior believe that there are steps that can be taken to improve the present situation and that the apparent trend isn't irreversible. Consultants such as Cheffers, Meehan and Goldaber have remarkably similar ideas about corrective and preventive actions. Though they use different terminology, they have developed similar models describing various states of crowd psychology. These range from controlled to explosive. When by reason of panic, anger or exuberance a crowd comes to this latter condition, it's so dangerous and destructive that nothing much can be done beyond calling riot police or troops to quell the violence. Therefore, the aim of controllers should be to keep things below the explosive level, and if the atmosphere approaches that, to make use of what Goldaber calls "defusing mechanisms."

The most commonly recommended measure is to improve facilities to lessen environmental irritations in crowd situations. Places that are clean, comfortable and convenient tend to promote good behavior. Even the illusion that management is concerned with the amenities seems to have a good effect. Goldaber advises clients, not entirely facetiously, that if they have only $50 for crowd-control innovations, they should employ two men, dress them in immaculate white coats, give them brooms and set them to furiously and conspicuously sweeping. Whether they sweep up any dirt is beside the point.

Last fall, Cheffers attended a Monday-night Patriots game at Schaefer Stadium. He's a big, beefy man, but even so found himself uneasy in the midst of bands of drunken, truculent, orgiastic fans roaming about in shadowy parking lots, reeking corridors and grimy stands. Following his field trip he submitted a detailed report to the Patriots, with suggestions for improvements. He thought "animalistic behavior" could be reduced if the joint—he called the parking lot Grub City—was cleaned up, smelled sweeter and was better lit. He felt there was great need to improve access to the parking and concession areas to cut down on jostling and long, frustrating lines. Hundreds of fans gathered hours before the game in parking lot "wastelands," where they had little to do but mill about, drink and start trouble. He thought that prettifying the lots, putting in some picnic and play areas, with room to throw Frisbees and balls around, might be worth a try. Among other things, Cheffers is very big on flowers as crowd controllers. "We will jump over ropes, knock down barricades, tear up lawns," he says, "but it takes a lot to make us walk through a flower bed." Cheffers believes that judiciously planted hardy annuals can do much to keep crowds where they are wanted and subliminally to remind them of their manners.

The Patriots, with the benefit of advice from both Cheffers and Goldaber, are now in the process of spending $5.8 million to upgrade Schaefer Stadium. "Generally, we want to make it an attractive place. We want good fans," says Sullivan. "Security and crowd control are not the only factors, but they are important ones."

Today, the idea of staging a major sporting event without dozens of law-and-order officers on hand is unthinkable. (On game day at Schaefer Stadium the security force, in or out of uniform, numbers more than 250.) However, security forces are often part of the fan-violence problem, not the solution to it. By tradition there is a certain anti-authoritarian spirit in sporting crowds, and this can be inflamed by rude, belligerent or even overly conspicuous cops. "When a guard ejects a fan, *who* is getting booed?" Goldaber asks. "Invariably, it's the guard." Goldaber thinks there's a need, not necessarily for larger security forces, but those that are better trained and more inclined to calm spectators by means other than busting them. Employing the 20 unarmed, ununiformed, fairly cool football players to patrol Fenway is seen as a step in the right direction.

Like everyone else, unruly spectators buy tickets, and promoters not wanting to offend them are inclined to tolerate behavior that wouldn't be permitted outside the stadium. Cheffers feels this is shortsighted. He thinks crowd controllers should be trained to spot troublemakers before they reach the explosive stage and to remove them quickly. Fans who are repeat offenders should be suspended for misconduct, as players are, and barred from attending games for a period of time. He agrees that the ejection should be accomplished as gently and unobtrusively as possible so as not to rile other spectators, but that the policy should be publicized and firmly carried out. Some customers might be lost, he admits, but their loss would be more than compensated for because new and better fans would be attracted by the improved conditions.

The link between hooliganism and alcohol consumption is as obvious as the reasons that sporting entrepreneurs have been loath to face up to this problem. Perhaps one of the best indications of serious concern about fan misbehavior is the new willingness to cut down on the beer and booze trade. In the last several years a dozen or so major stadiums and arenas have taken steps to halt sales before the latter part of a game and to restrict sales in certain particularly rowdy sections or the amounts individual fans can buy. There's even occasional talk of eliminating beer concessions entirely. For example, Sullivan says the Patriots "had considered" such a drastic move at Schaefer Stadium, even though it's named for a brewery, which reportedly paid a million dollars for the honor.

Perhaps the boldest action of this sort has been taken by the Chicago White Sox. According to Schaffer, the Comiskey Park security chief, when new ownership acquired the Sox in 1981, it was alarmed at the amount of violence in the park and Comiskey's steadily deteriorating reputation. In an effort to improve things, all hard-liquor sales were banned inside the stadium. The Sox estimate this cost them about $100,000 but that it has had a calming effect on crowd behavior and made security enforcement, for which the White Sox now pay about $300,000 a season, much easier.

Sports have been successful in developing techniques that move spectators toward rather than away from explosive states. Again, nobody wants them actually to blow up, just to come close to the exhilarating flash point. "It's good business for the teams to psych up a crowd," says Goldaber. "We talk about killer instincts, rivalries. You give the wrong guy a rivalry, give him people around him who are raucous, contributing to the steam-up, and you may well have a dangerous problem."

The statement of the problem more or less indicates the solution. What Goldaber calls the hype and hoopla needs to be toned down, and reality—that these are games, not genuine confrontations of world-shaking significance—must be emphasized. The participants, from management to coaches to players, are in the best position to deliver this message and make it believable in the stands. "Unwarranted behaviors"—such as on-the-field fights, tantrums and the like, which Cheffers has found are so likely to incite spectators—need to be eliminated, not just mildly rebuked or penalized. Goldaber also believes players should be instructed and encouraged to display pacific behavior and to make more gestures of what used to be referred to as sportsmanship—pre-game handshakes, etc.

"When a lineman hits the quarterback," says Goldaber, "the crowd is going to yell for a roughing-the-passer call. But if the lineman reaches down and yanks up the guy he just hit and pats him on the back, and they both run back to their huddles, that's something I call a sociological signal to the crowd that this is just a game. Those fans who feel they're in a war will be calmed by the gesture."

Cheffers also feels that efforts must be made to educate or re-educate fans. "I care about this," he says, "because I'm one of those who think that sport can and should have a very constructive influence on society. I would say that the greatest value of sporting competition is that it teaches us how to handle winning and losing without becoming antisocial. When what's achieved predominates over how it's achieved, then a disrespect for the entire game, the entire sport, ensues. Violence follows disrespect. The fearful thing is that what we are now being taught to respect is violence. Sport is making it fashionable."

BLOOD IN THE STANDS[3]

The trouble began in Section Y on the northeast end of Heysel Stadium in Brussels. In the stands thousands of fans were waiting for the opening of the European Cup Final between Britain's Liverpool and Italy's Juventus of Turin. About 45 minutes before the scheduled 8:15 p.m. kickoff, the mostly young Liverpool fans began to taunt the Juventus followers. Emboldened by alcohol, many backed up their insults by hurling rocks and bottles over the wire fence that separated them from the Italians. Suddenly, as if acting on some invisible signal, the screaming British crowd exploded across the standing-room terraces. They swarmed into the adjoining section, heaving rocks and bottles. The human tide crushed and maimed people in scenes of sheerest horror. Television cameras provided watching millions with close-up pictures of fans caught beneath a human pile; of hands held out in vain supplication; of the injured and dying crying out pitifully for help.

By the time the riot had subsided and the wave of raw violence had passed, 38 people lay dead; more than 400 had been injured. Amid the scene of death and destruction, people wandered aimlessly about the field, injured and in shock. "I've seen too much," moaned one bloodied Italian fan, tears streaming down his cheeks. "I've seen death."

The 30th annual playing of the European final was one of the bloodiest sporting events in modern memory. It outraged Europeans and raised agonizing questions about why Europe's soccer stadiums are increasingly coming to resemble gladiator pits. The behavior of the English fans, who were blamed for starting the

[3]Reprint of a magazine article by staff writer Richard Lacayo and staff reporters. *Time*. 125:38+. Je. 10, '85. Copyright © 1985 Time Inc. All rights reserved. Reprinted by permission from *Time*.

riot, resulted in much soul searching in Britain about why a land famous for patience and civility produces the most violent soccer crowds. A shocked and angry Prime Minister Margaret Thatcher declared that the country was "worse than numb" over the riot. Said she: "Those responsible have brought shame and disgrace to their country."

The rampage began as 60,000 spectators were filling the 55-year-old stadium, five miles from the center of Brussels, to witness one of the premier events of the international soccer calendar. An estimated 400 million viewers in Europe and Africa were tuned in for what promised to be a feast of first-class football, as soccer is known outside North America. Many of the Liverpudlians, dressed in the bright red colors of their home team, were gathered in Section Y, separated by a flimsy wire fence and a stairway from the mostly Italian spectators in Section Z, an uncovered sloping stand. The Liverpudlians, many of them drunk, began pushing against the fence. Suddenly, weakened by the weight of several hundred heaving bodies, the divider collapsed. "It was like watching guerrillas in a battle," recalled Giampietro Donamigo, an Italian fan. "They came forward in waves toward the fence, throwing bottles. . . . Some answered back with threats, but most of us were terrified. We tried to move away."

As the Liverpool crowd poured across the stand, the Juventus fans panicked. Hundreds made a rush for the nearest exit, beyond a low wall at the bottom of the sloping spectator terrace. Some managed to clamber over the wall, dropping to the ground on the other side. Hundreds more were trapped, crushed by the weight of the crowd. Then, with a sickening crack, the concrete wall collapsed, killing some and spilling others onto the field in a murderous cascade of bodies and fractured concrete.

"There was a mass of crushed bodies," said Renzo Rocchetti, a Juventus supporter from Milan. "I saw people trampled to death under the feet of the frightened mob, stepping on their bodies, including many babies and children." Remarked an off-duty British policeman among the Liverpool supporters: "Those poor bloody Italians went down like a pack of cards."

Most of the 1,000 Belgian police assigned to the game were outside, trying to control drunken groups still attempting to pour into the stadium. Inside, helmeted Red Cross medics dodged bricks, bottles and smoke bombs as they worked among the dying and injured, frantically trying to resuscitate people who had been suffocated beneath piles of bodies. It was 30 minutes before ambulances arrived, and at first the dead were carried out of the stadium on sections of crowd-control barriers, some covered with flags and banners that only minutes earlier had been waved by cheering fans. The dead, their faces and limbs a grotesque purple, were taken to a makeshift mortuary outside the stadium, where priests administered the last rites.

In Turin, the home city of at least 10,000 Juventus supporters in Brussels, there was an outpouring of grief. Among the dead was restaurant owner Giovacchino Landini, 49. "Why did it have to be him?" cried his daughter Monica, 22. "He was too passionately fond of Juventus." Of the dead, 31 were Italians, including a ten-year-old boy and a woman. Also killed were four Belgians, two Frenchmen and a Briton who was a resident of Brussels. All the dead were asphyxiated or crushed. Ten spectators, all British, were arrested, none for alleged offenses committed inside the stadium.

Fearful of triggering an even more terrible riot if they called off the match, Belgian officials and members of the Union of European Football Associations decided that it should be played. "Call it a surrender to fear if you wish," said Association Treasurer Jo Van Marle. Italian Prime Minister Benedetto ("Bettino") Craxi, in Moscow for discussions with Soviet Leader Mikhail Gorbachev, telephoned Belgian Prime Minister Wilfried Martens after the riot to protest the decision. Said Martens: "I told him that the decision to begin play was taken purely for reasons of security." The crowd, which was largely unaware of the magnitude of the tragedy, watched the macabre match as helmeted riot-control police stood guard and ambulance sirens wailed. (For the record, Juventus won, 1–0, with a penalty kick in the 58th minute of play.)

Across Europe, along with the grief and shock, came the recriminations. In an editorial, the *Times* of London declared: "It is hard to resist the conclusion that the game of soccer is as good as dead." Some laid the blame for the Brussels tragedy squarely on the estimated 16,000 Liverpool followers at the match. Many had spent the afternoon before the game drinking in the streets and bars of Brussels. The Belgian government acted swiftly by banning all British teams—from England, Wales, Scotland and Northern Ireland—from competing in Belgium "until further notice." England's Football Association then announced that it was withdrawing all English soccer teams from European competition for the season starting in September. "It is absolutely unbearable to continue to admit the English hordes on soccer grounds," said Jean-Michel Fournet-Fayard, president of the French Football Federation.

While not underplaying the responsibility of the British fans for the tragedy, commentators and sports officials charged that Belgian police had been lax in preparing for the possibility of violence, especially considering the reputation of British club followers. (Last year, for example, an English fan was killed by an irate bar owner and 141 were arrested in disturbances connected with a match in Brussels.) The police were also criticized for not segregating the fans of the opposing teams more effectively and for not searching more thoroughly for weapons as the crowd entered Heysel Stadium. Others claimed that there had been too few police on hand, even though 1,000 would seem to be adequate by the standards of most sports events. To many watching the rampage on television, the police in the stadium appeared somewhat lame and ineffectual. Said one Liverpool fan: "The police were just too scared."

Soccer, the world's most popular sport, for decades has unleashed ferocious scenes. In 1945 George Orwell, deploring the bloodlust of soccer crowds, wrote that "serious sport" is "war minus the shooting." In Lima in 1964, some 300 spectators were killed in riots sparked by a disputed referee's call. In China, where civil disorder is rare, hundreds of fans rioted in the streets of Peking last month after the home team was knocked out of the World Cup by Hong Kong. Even as crowds were headed for the stadium in Brussels, families in Mexico City were mourning the victims of a stadium riot last week in which eight people, two of them children, were crushed to death.

The penchant of English fans for rock-hurling mayhem has become an increasing problem at home, and one of the country's sorriest exports. In the past three months alone, England has witnessed three major soccer riots that have left one dead and scores injured. At matches abroad, rampaging fans have become ambassadors of bad will, bashing heads in France, trading tear-gas volleys with police in Italy and urinating on spectators in Spain. In 1975 Leeds United, a team whose followers have one of the worst reputations, was barred from playing on the Continent for four years after Leeds fans raised a storm of violence at the European Cup Final in Paris. In 1977 Manchester United was briefly kicked out of the European Cup Winners competition after its fans rioted during a first-round match in St. Etienne, France.

Prime Minister Thatcher responded to the violence in Brussels by summoning a number of her country's football officials to confer with her on the problem of fan violence. She announced that Britain would be contributing $317,500 to a special fund for victims of the riot and families of the dead. Last March, Thatcher set up a panel that included members of her cabinet to study soccer violence after fans went on a rampage in Luton, England. The Prime Minister said last week that she will now meet sooner than planned with the group to review progress on implementing some of the measures that have already been agreed to, including a voluntary ban by clubs on the sale of alcohol in stadiums. A similar measure has led to a sharp decrease in violent episodes over the past five years in Scotland, where soccer brawls were once a favorite pastime. Faced with declining attendance and rising demands for expensive security precautions, team owners in England have so far been unwilling to give up the revenues from drink concessions. Now that the teams are banned from European competition, their losses are certain to be even greater.

Stadium design has also been cited as a reason for the frequency of English soccer violence. Trouble at games often starts among the working-class youths who fill up the low-cost, standing-room areas known as terraces, similar to the areas occupied by the Liverpool and Juventus fans in the Brussels stadium. Sir Philip Goodhart, a Conservative Member of Parliament, believes that one reason there is less fan mayhem at sporting events in the U.S., a nation that many Britons regard as violence prone, is that its stadiums have fewer standing-room sections. Says Goodhart: "It is very difficult to riot when you are sitting down."

To be sure, there are those who feel the soccer violence is largely a symptom of deeper social and economic problems, perhaps even a direct result of Britain's 13.5% unemployment rate. In Liverpool, for example, 25% of the labor force is out of work. "We have football," says psychologist Peter Marsh. "Other societies have street gangs." A 1980 study of soccer hooliganism in Britain found that four-fifths of those charged with soccer-related crimes were either unemployed or manual workers. Says sociologist John Williams of the University of Leicester: "We must go into the community to find out why young people find status in this kind of violence."

A different picture of some soccer rowdies emerged two weeks ago in a British courtroom, where 25 supporters of Cambridge United were sentenced to prison terms of up to five years for soccer-related assaults. Members of a "hooligan army," as they were called by the press, they were organized into a paramilitary group and were affluent enough to buy "uniforms" consisting of costly designer sweaters, jeans and track shoes. Indeed, much of the trouble at soccer games seems to be started by similarly well-organized gangs of about 200 members that attach themselves to their home teams. Many of the groups have their own chants, symbols and even weapons of choice. The infamous Bushwackers of Millwall, a tattered docklands area of London, wear surgical masks during matches to hide their identities and favor small Stanley cutting tools to carry out their assaults. Some Liverpool supporters who attended the Brussels game insist that many fans dressed in the crimson of Liverpool spoke in the Cockney accents of Chelsea and West Ham, London neighborhoods whose clubs are known for their marauding followers. In fact, Liverpool fans had a reputation among the British for relative propriety.

As the search for causes of the violence in Brussels went on, those touched by the tragedy made an effort to come to terms with their feelings. At a Requiem Mass held in Liverpool's Roman Catholic cathedral, the Archbishop of Liverpool, Derek Worlock, summed up the feelings of shocked and puzzled citizens. "If it comes to responsible human conduct and moral behavior," he said, "the answer lies in ourselves." At a service held in a hangar at a Brussels military airport on Saturday, Belgian Prime Minister Martens paid his final respects to 25 of the riot victims. He spoke of the need "to put an end to this mad race toward violence." Then, as more than 100 relatives of the dead tearfully filed past the coffins covered with flowers, three priests gave their blessings. Unless ways are found to ensure that such tragedies do not recur, those flowers could become a memorial for European soccer itself.

IV. THE 1984 SUMMER OLYMPIC GAMES

EDITOR'S INTRODUCTION

The Olympic Games are in many ways a microcosm of the world of sport. Held up as an ideal—the peaceful assembly of athletes from around the globe for the purpose of honorable competition—they suffer from all the ills of modern sports events: cheating through the use of drugs, manipulation by commercial interests, inflation of winners to the status of instant celebrities, flagrant violation of rules dividing amateurs from professionals. Worst of all, the Games have been compromised by politics: judges are notoriously biased, and each of the last three Olympiads was marred by a boycott instituted by some countries to protest the social policies or military activities of others. Yet the Olympics retain their reputation as the ultimate sports festival, a celebration of athletic excellence that captures the attention of millions of people, including many who never take an interest in any other sports event.

The United States has for years been a major contender in the Olympics, maintaining a symbolic rivalry with the Soviet Union and its allies. In the summer of 1984, four years after American athletes were withdrawn from the Moscow summer Olympic Games by President Carter for political reasons, the United States hosted the Games at Los Angeles. Despite a retaliatory boycott by the Soviet-bloc countries, more nations participated in this Olympics than in any previous one.

As Roger Rosenblatt points out in his paean to the Olympics, the 1984 Summer Games were marked by a uniquely American combination of aggressive capitalism, irrepressible hero worship, and exhibitionistic patriotism. The organizing committee's application of high-technology solutions to the problems of drug detection and subjective judging is described by Alvin P. Sanoff. Pete Axthelm examines the extent to which commercialism has altered the character of the Games and detects "a fine line between progress and corruption," adding: "Actually, hypocrisy and fantasy have always been combined in the Olympic rings." Finally, Leonard Koppett offers a series of suggestions for improvement of the Games, an answer both to critics who want to see the Games dismantled and to exploiters who profit from the status quo.

WHY WE PLAY THESE GAMES[1]

Eight thousand banners, did you say? Covering 120 miles of Los Angeles? Hanging from 300 different types of lampposts? O.K. Some of the brackets for the banners had to be different too; a real headache. Certainly not, you wouldn't want to use just any colors. Had to be magenta, vermilion, chrome yellow, violet, aqua. "Festive Federalism," the designers call it. (What does that mean?) Oh, sorry. Please go on. You were talking about construction: 3,500 construction workers at 67 different sites, including Olympic Villages, places for the Games, training facilities, parking lots. That is, if the cars can get there. Gridlock city, eh? No! Fifty-two miles of chain-link fence? Well, you can't be too careful. By all means, read the grocery list for the athletes. Pork, 63,700 lbs.; beef, 206,555 lbs.; 70,000 dozen eggs. (You *do* deliver?) You say that if someone laid those eggs end to end they'd stretch for 25 miles? One pooped chicken. That's a joke, son. No harm, no foul.

But where is the center of this thing? No, not the $525 million budget or the anticipated infusion of $3.3 billion into the local economy or the 269,000 dozen cookies. One million new trees planted by a conservation group? Good for them. Nothing like a tree. The question is why. Why, as the magenta was going up at the Los Angeles Coliseum, were 7,800 athletes from 140 nations loading their gear and kissing Mother goodbye? Numbers? Here's a number. On July 28, 2 billion people of the great trembling bipolar world will lay down their washing and watch these Games. Why?

[1]Reprint of a magazine article by Roger Rosenblatt, senior writer. *Time.* 124:34–7. Jl. 30, '84. Copyright © 1984 Time Inc. All rights reserved. Reprinted by permission from *Time.*

Looking mighty Establishment in his white open-collar shirt and navy-blue suit, John Carlos sits at a table in the headquarters of the Los Angeles Olympic Organizing Committee, where he now works. Behind one shoulder the American flag, behind the other the Olympic. But for a bum ankle, he says, he could still tear up the track. The last time we saw John Carlos was 1968 on a podium in Mexico City, standing in the grainy evening light rigid as an exclamation point. The black-power salute; an antique of the '60s. He is speaking of something else:

"I was a fair-to-exciting swimmer. I guess I put as much ener-gy into swimming at that age ten] as I ever did into track and field. I wanted to swim the English Channel. I told my father: I want to know something about this English Channel. Why are these people swimming it? How does one swim with, you know, the sharks? How do swimmers go to the bathroom? What happens in the night? And then I learned about the Olympic Games. And I said: Oh, wow. I'd like to do *that*.

"Then I started to ask more questions about swimming. And my father pulled me aside, and he said: Look. Swimming is a bad way to go. You have to be in the water at least six, seven hours a day. He said: Where would you train? You can't train in the Harlem River; you lose seven or eight guys a year drowning, which is true. And he said you can't go to the ocean. The water's too rough. He said you can't go to the public pool; everybody's try-ing to cool off. Everything he said made sense. So I started to walk off like with my lip stuck out. And he tapped me on the shoulder and he said: Look, man, the heaviest hasn't come yet. They have private clubs, but you can't join any of them. And I said: Why? Because we can't afford it? He said no. Because you're colored; they won't let you in. So I walked off in a kind of mystic mood, dejected but not dejected. My old man looked at me and asked: Well, what you going to do? You gonna quit? Just look around and find something else."

Where is the center of this thing? A man who learned how fast his legs could move because as a boy he outran cops in Harlem, who worked out in cordovan shoes on the F.D.R. Drive because his father was a cobbler and cordovans *last*? Does one watch the Olympics to see a spectacle of individuals? A festival of nerve?

Perhaps something collective as well. *Something*. America bursts into song at the torch relay, and 7 million tickets go on sale.

But they said the boycott would kill the Games. Evidently not. No boycott has done real damage; not the U.S. boycott in 1980 or that of the Africans in 1976 or of some Arab states in 1956 in response to the crisis over Suez. As for this year of Soviet revenge, not only are more nations than ever sending delegations, but people are saying that the Games may be better off without an East-West brawl. Quieter countries will get a chance to strut.

But they said commercialism would kill the Games. Hardly. In a world where weapons are sold like hot cakes, who really worries about getting and spending at a sports event? To the contrary, the commercialism feels right, at least it does for the U.S. Competition in the Games, competition around them. Ever see an amateur capitalist?

So Botswana, a land so arid that its currency is called rain, proudly sends a yachtsman to represent the nation. And Israel cheers 30 athletes and promises 1,000 tourists, though the country has yet to win a single medal. This will be Communist China's first major presence in the Olympics; they are bringing a contingent of 353. Egypt and Italy will be sending the largest delegations they have ever sent. Singapore wouldn't miss it; except for boycotting in 1980, that country has participated in every Olympics since 1948.

Even war does not get in the way. Lebanon sends (fittingly) a team of skeet and trapshooters. (On the TV news recently, the shooters complained—seriously—that they were not getting enough practice.) The Irelands unite North and South for a moment to create a single team. Astonishingly, the Koreans considered doing the same. They matter, these Games: to Belgium's cyclists, Argentina's single sculler, Holland's swimmers, the boxers from the Seychelles. India's field hockey team is out to prove something against Pakistan. Kenya's long-distance runners have things to prove to themselves. Cheers for the Chadians. Hail to the Swazis. Where else would these people come together so eagerly? Not the U.N.

Is this the center, then? An international Woodstock? "The Olympic flame is the only hope for brotherhood, understanding and dialogue," says Juan Antonio Samaranch, president of the International Olympic Committee. What else would he say? "The Olympics are the only times in the history of the world when so many nations come together in one spot in an association of friendship," says Charles Palmer, president of the British Olympic Association. Vested interest. According to Kurthan Fisek, a professor of public management from the University of Ankara, "No single institution in the entire history of mankind has been able to equate itself with world peace as effectively and consistently." Let's not get carried away.

Yet not all of this is cant. Michael Jordan of the U.S. team pretends not to see the basket, then lunges toward it, as if stumbling on the court. Suddenly he leaps, glides, hangs in the air. The ball is cradled in the palm of his hand at the side of his head. Still flying, he flicks his wrist forward, as if waving hello, and the ball sets off on a flight of its own. When the hoop is scored, Jordan is airborne still. Why are we pleased?

Heroes must be part of the answer. There are those like Jordan, Mary Decker, Carl Lewis who enter the Olympics with greatness already thrust upon them; one will test their performances against their reputations. Better still, sudden heroes always seem to emerge and establish themselves, often in sports one has dismissed as boring or has paid no attention to before. Olga Korbut and Nadia Comaneci created gymnastics for most Americans, not because Americans never heard of gymnastics, but because they had not seen the sport performed by virtuosos. A subtle surprise of the Olympics is how individuals can transform the events in which they participate. Boxing enrages and disgusts you. Then Sugar Ray Leonard skips into the ring, and the sport is God and country.

Much of the appeal of the Olympics centers on individual heroes, yet heroism in the Games is lightweight; it bears none of the mythic armor of professional sports. With professional athletes, allegories develop with the records; Mantle was pain, Unitas skill, Ali poetry and power. The Olympic Games are too brief for spectators to construct a folklore. Personalities like Nadia float to the top for a few days, but only as they are attached to performances.

The hero and the act are one. If an allegorical hero is to be found in the Games, it is youth in general. A time of life is held still. For two weeks nothing ages; at least that is the illusion. The Olympics make the illusion grand. All the world agrees to it.

Individuals compete with one another; that accounts for the Games' appeal as well. Some athletes claim to be oblivious of the competition, but the audience never is. One need not argue the merits of winning or playing the game. The fact is that the sight of someone winning is a pleasurable thing. A rarity of the times, it is clean and unambiguous. So is losing. In any Olympic event there is at least one athlete who does not expect to lose. Not *she*. She has never lost. Yet she will lose today. She will pit her enormous will against her battered body, and come in second, third or ninth. One looks for the shock on her face, beneath the fatigue or despair. The shock is everyone's.

Individuals also compete against themselves, and the selves are complicated. "More than an athlete, I'm a human being," said John Carlos. "I have emotions, needs, wants. I got the whole shot." In every volleyball game, in every foot race one sees the whole shot: mind over matter, mind over mind. John Landy turns his head; Roger Bannister shoots by. On the field it often seems more than a struggle for victory; it seems a struggle for a place in the world, self-assertion through combat. Sometimes it looks sublime—in a dive off the 10-meter platform, on the parallel bars. Sometimes it looks dispassionately cruel. Either way the struggle wins the affection of the crowd, which sees in the exercise of discipline a morality play not necessarily related to sports. Throats go dry merely because a fellow human being is doing all that is remotely possible.

For Americans these demonstrations of will connect with their history, or at least they feel that they connect with their history, which comes to the same thing. Everything Americans wish to believe about their national character is housed in sports: vitality, spontaneity, the bursting of bonds. No state religion for the U.S., but sports will do as well. The Puritans condemned games as antispiritual. Their heirs retaliated by fusing holidays with tournaments—football on Thanksgiving, basketball at Christmas—all blasphemies culminating in Super Sunday. Thorstein Veblen contended that sports and religion have the same genesis in a basic "belief in an inscrutable propensity or a preternatural interposition in the sequence of events." We'll take his word for it. In simpler terms, Americans make stadiums their churches because they trust that therein lies national virtue. Extolling baseball, Albert Spalding, the sporting-goods king, called the game "the exponent of American Courage, Confidence, Combativeness; American Dash, Discipline, Determination; American Energy, Eagerness, Enthusiasm; American Pluck, Persistency, Performance; American Spirit, Sagacity, Success; American Vim, Vigor, Vitality." Only real piety could inspire such alliteration.

Whatever else, these displays of individual worth are simply beautiful. In a way, the Games extend definitions of beauty. Why is synchronized swimming no more beautiful than the bulging grimace of a weight lifter? Art rarely pins these things down. Painters miss it. Writers do worse, with exceptions such as Mailer on boxing, Updike on golf, Hemingway on a bobsled run: "A bob shot past, all the crew moving in time, and as it rushed at express train speed for the first turn, the crew all cried 'Ga-a-a-a-r!' and the bob roared in an icy smother around the curve and dropped off down the glassy run below." The *ands* do it. Everything must keep moving. Housman celebrated an "athlete dying young" because the boy would never have to learn that eventually things slow down, grow old, stop.

The beauty is motion, and motion does not last. Most things ephemeral have limited appeal, but the heart of the Olympics is that things shine for a moment and no more. Did Dwight Stones really clear that bar at 7 ft. 8 in.? One saw it happen a second ago. One saw it again on instant replay. Yet the jump no longer exists, nor can it return. Billy Mills, who won the 10,000-meter run in Tokyo, said, "For one fleeting moment an athlete will know he or she is the best in the world. Then the moment is gone." Bill Russell, pro basketball's philosopher, likes the short-term nature of sports because it bespeaks a world of reasonable expectations. "Sports not only claims small bits of time," says Russell, "it also claims smaller bits of truth. . . . The only truth [sports] claims is the score." Since nothing lasts, pleasure relies on memory. It is not the feats that are preserved but the joy.

Beauty also seems inseparable from excellence. Often the Games provide more than excellence, since mere proficiency presumes existing standards of performance, and some athletes set wholly new standards. "I began to run slowly," Jesse Owens recalled. "Then faster, gaining speed with each step. My legs were moving at top speed now. I came closer and closer to the takeoff board. At the last moment I shortened my stride and hit the board with a pounding right foot. I felt my body rise in the air, and I scissors-kicked at the peak of it, flying 15, then 20, then 25 ft. through the air—straining closer and closer to the towel. And then I landed—past it!"

Reasons to do with individuals, reasons to do with nations. Ever since the Soviets announced their boycott, there has been much talk of holding a nationless Olympics, individuals competing as individuals alone. Such a plan is unlikely to work; people would identify athletes by nationality no matter what colors they wore. In fact, nationalism seems an attraction, not an impediment to the Games. People belong to nations as to families. Things only sour when nationalism brings intentions outside sports. When the Russians bloodied the Hungarians in a water-polo match in 1956, one was not witnessing nationalism but war.

But much importance is given to mere participation. Governments spend a great deal of money and effort for no purpose but showing up, for taking a place in a community of nations. Many African nations see the Games as a chance to become part of international sports. Carlos Giron, a diver from Mexico, views it wider: "You feel like a citizen of the world." Mohammed Abdel Meguid Mohyeldin, secretary-general of the Egyptian Olympic Committee, believes that "participation shows you are interested in humanity, not merely sports."

Such interest creates not one spectacle but two: the spectacle of the Games and that of those watching them. If television cameras had a "reverse gear" that could be applied from country to country, one might see quite a show of Peruvians, Thais and Iowans privately gasping and clapping as they watch the action. Excessive communications are said to work against human feelings, but here the effect is the opposite. Not a show of world peace, perhaps, but something valuable, nonetheless, in a shared set of relatively benign emotions on so vast a scale.

Yet the feelings are not entirely formless, either. There are very few historical experiences that the world holds in common. The Olympic Games are one. "A tradition," says George Liveris, president of the Greek Shooting Federation, and once an Olympic participant. "They are the longest lasting social activity that exists." Maybe that accounts for the remarkable success of the American torch relay. On the roads, the cheers for the torchbearers came out sounding like old-fashioned patriotism, but the impulse seemed to go both broader and deeper, to a connection with Greece, with the past, with everyone's past.

Perhaps this connection is tied to the dreams of peaceful coexistence that the Games seem to promote. "The ideological differences between the Greeks of Sparta and Athens were fully as profound as those between the Soviet Union and the United States today," says historian and journalist I. F. Stone. "Nevertheless the Games provided the chief Pan Hellenic festival at which all Hellenic peoples came together under a kind of truce on war and politics." No sports fan, by his own admission, and no cockeyed optimist either, Stone nonetheless sees the early Games as "a symbol of badly needed unity among the peoples, just as the Olympic Games today could be a symbol of unity among all members of the human race." The question is what power such a symbol has, and how long its effects survive. It is easy to point to the 1,503-year hiatus between Emperor Theodosius' suspension and Baron De Coubertin's resuscitation of the Games and conclude that the world did not need them, but the world has only painted itself into its deadly corner in the past 40 years. If, as Stone says, the Games really are a symbol of the "human fraternity," who these days would remove such a symbol?

Or is the appeal of the Games simpler than all this? What one has here, after all, are simple contests, simple consequences, the simple delight of observers at basic human activities. Remove the 8,000 banners, the 52 miles of fencing, and the scene is pastoral. Someone jumps or throws a discus. Someone swims. People play ball. Close out the noise, remove the fancy equipment, and one could feel that the Games show the world rediscovering itself in

absolute serenity and innocence. Nothing is supposed to be innocent any more, of course, but it is hard to read corruption in the
400-meter freestyle.

In a few days, gridlock. Los Angeles airport will quake with
arriving jets. The freeways will turn to stone. Athletes will start
digging into the 70,000 dozen eggs. The 3,500 construction workers, having put up the bleachers and the Styrofoam signs, will relax at home, ready to watch ABC's closeups and moments of
Olympic history and expert analyses. No, the hotel never got your
reservation. Sorry, this ticket is good only for the first round of
archery. The world will look at California, which in turn will look
as laid back as Edvard Munch's *The Scream*. Yet the place should
survive. For the moment there is a mixture of frenzy, anticipation
and smog. This Saturday the final torchbearer will be prepared
to do the final leg, the name of the runner kept secret till the last
minute by L.A.O.O.C. President Peter Ueberroth, who, after five
years of haggling, deserves some fun.

Henry David Thoreau (second cousin three times removed)
is sitting in the Los Angeles Coliseum watching the U.S. pigeon
team peck away at the grass. The Games are 23 days away. Thoreau is the Olympic commissioner of track and field. Good-
natured to his toes, he looks like everyone's favorite ice-cream
man. His seat overlooks the finish line, where all the races will
end. Below and around him, workers hammer and drill in preparation for the opening ceremonies. A theater; a set going up. The
gateways to the seats have been painted magenta, vermilion,
chrome yellow, violet and aqua. The sky is merely blue. Is track
and field the center of the Olympics, Mr. Thoreau? Definitely.
"Everyone can understand it."

His second cousin three times removed was all for things readily understood. "Simplify the problem of life, distinguish the necessary and the real. Probe the earth and see where your main roots
run." On a wall outside the Coliseum, the motto of the Games:
CITIUS, ALTIUS, FORTIUS—faster, higher, stronger. Simplify the problem. Now the workers are washing the track. A light breeze swirls
in the vast cone. Suds fill the lanes where the kids will run.

HOW THEY'RE KEEPING THE OLYMPICS HONEST[2]

Officials in Los Angeles are going all out to make sure that the Summer Olympics will be the fairest in history.

To prevent controversies such as those that marred past contests, organizers are taking steps ranging from rotating practice sites so that no team has a training advantage to planning bus schedules so carefully that no athlete will miss an event because of traffic.

Yet the top priority in this year's events is cracking down on drug use.

"What we want is a drug-free Olympics where everyone competes and does his best," says Dr. Tony Daly, medical director of the Los Angeles games.

Barely a week before the start of the games, three members of the Yugoslav Olympic team, whom officials would not name, failed drug tests and were not allowed to go to Los Angeles.

Still another controversial case developed just days before the opening. After winning a race at the Coors International Bicycling Classic in Colorado on July 18, U.S. cyclist Alexi Grewal drew a suspension when tests proved positive for a stimulant common in cold remedies and in some herbal teas. That penalty, which would have kept him out of the Olympics, was soon lifted because officials felt that the test, performed in Denver, did not precisely identify what he had taken.

At the Olympics, officials have set up a 2-million-dollar "state of the art" drug-testing laboratory—the only one of its kind in the U.S.

Located on the campus of the University of California at Los Angeles, the lab is analyzing urine samples of the top four finishers in each event, plus those of other competitors selected at random. In team sports, testing of the members on winning squads is entirely random.

[2]Reprint of an article by Alvin P. Sanoff, senior editor for social trends, and staff reporters. *U. S. News & World Report.* 97:25–6. Ag. 6, '84. Copyright © 1984 by U. S. News & World Report, Inc. Reprinted by permission.

Technicians are taking aim at scores of banned drugs. Among them: Codeine, anabolic steroids, amphetamines and even some over-the-counter remedies for colds, hay fever and other allergies.

In all, some 1,500 athletes—about 20 percent of those competing—will be checked, with the lab averaging one test every 5 minutes round the clock.

Tests are completed within 24 hours, and if the results show the presence of a banned drug, then a second sample, taken at the same time as the first, is checked in the presence of the athlete and medical representatives from his or her delegation. The second analysis is final, and those found guilty will be stripped of any medals. In team competition, a positive test will mean forfeit of a game.

The lab equipment being used is so sensitive that it can pick up 1 part in a billion, explains Daly. If a cube of sugar were dissolved in a swimming pool, for example, the equipment could detect it.

Officials hope that the mere existence of the tests will discourage drug use. "The athletes know we mean business," comments Kim Jasper, director of doping control for the Los Angeles Olympic Organizing Committee (LAOOC). "They know they will be caught if they take something."

Still, knowledgeable sources say that some athletes, possibly with expert help, may be trying to beat the tests. Some are reported to be taking growth hormone, for which no tests have yet been devised. Others may be consuming a synthetic form of the natural hormone testosterone, a banned anabolic steroid.

"I suspect that some people who will be competing in the games have been using testosterone," says Dr. John Lombardo, a sports-medicine specialist at the Cleveland Clinic.

Physicians doubt that growth hormone aids athletic performance, but they say that testosterone, used most often by weight lifters and those in other strength sports, builds muscle mass and enhances aggressiveness. Both drugs have dangerous side effects. Growth hormone enlarges internal organs, while testosterone has been linked to liver damage and cardiovascular disease.

Behind the greater use of drugs in sports is the desire to win. "If you told an athlete that eating Brillo soap pads would help, you wouldn't find a clean pot within 200 miles," says Bob Goldman, author of *Death in the Locker Room,* which deals with use of anabolic steroids in sports.

Many athletes fall into the habit out of fear that competitors are taking drugs and gaining an edge. Over the years, athletes from Western nations and the Soviet bloc have pointed the finger at one another.

Although most experts favor tests to discourage such practices, Paul Ward, a U.S. discus and shot-put coach, calls the testing "Gestapo action." He argues that just as Prohibition didn't work with alcohol, it won't work with drugs. "It will drive people underground," says Ward.

At the Pan American Games last year in Caracas, tests detected 17 drug users among competitors, including two from the United States. Twelve U.S. track and field athletes withdrew before they could be checked, although one later returned and passed the test.

The ultimate solution, many experts say, does not lie in testing alone but in helping athletes use new discoveries in nutrition and biomechanics to boost performance. Dr. Irving Dardik, chairman of the U.S. Olympic Council on Sports Medicine, says athletes must be shown that there are better ways to get ahead than taking drugs.

Testing of another kind also is going on this year. Women have cells scraped from inside their mouths and examined to make sure they have two X chromosomes, which determine the female sex. Those with other chromosome combinations cannot compete. Such testing began after questions arose in the 1960s over the sex of some female athletes—most of them from the Soviet bloc.

Besides the latest in chemical tests, officials here also are confident that the games will feature the best available timing and photographic equipment for track, swimming, cycling and other events.

Particularly in swimming, the possibility of error by judges is small because the gun that signals the start of a race also triggers the timing equipment. When competitors touch a pad running along the wall of the pool at the end of the race, their time is automatically tallied.

Even with the most precise equipment, human beings will be called on to render decisions. In track, for example, judges have to examine the pictures of a photo finish and determine the winner.

"Somebody has to interpret what the technology tells them," says Michael Mount, LAOOC's group vice president for support operations.

In other sports, such as gymnastics and diving, winners are decided solely on the basis of the judges' scores. This year, however, the chief gymnastics judge will see all scores on a computer screen before they are posted. If one judge's score differs significantly from the scores of the others, he or she will be notified and have a chance to make an adjustment before scores are official.

Although most Soviet-bloc countries have boycotted the games, judges from those nations will be ruling on the results of some sports, such as boxing. This has led to protests from some U.S. athletes who fear that the judges will be prejudiced against Americans. Divers will be spared such controversy since neutral judges will be used for the final events.

Scheduling had been another problem at previous Olympics, but organizers say that this year competitors will have no excuse for missing events.

In addition to a fleet of 500 buses to move athletes around, other vehicles are available on a standby basis for emergencies. A network of several hundred traffic watchers will inform bus drivers of any tie-ups so that they can change their routes to get players to destinations on time.

Much planning also has gone into picking practice times and sites. A questionnaire asking information on preferred training locations was sent to every nation's Olympic committee. The results were fed into a computer, and a schedule was put together.

"We tried to rotate both time and place so that everybody had the same chance to train at the sites where the actual competition will occur," says Charles Cale, group vice president for sports at the LAOOC.

While complaints from athletes may well surface as the games unfold, officials here believe they have gone the extra mile to insure fairness—but there are limits. "No" was the answer to one team that asked for tea and biscuits to be served at their training site at a specific time of day. "That one, we couldn't work out," says Cale. "We suggested that they bring their own thermos bottles and biscuits."

MONEY AND HYPOCRISY[3]

Amid the assorted deadlines that preceded the opening of the Olympics, a significant one passed almost unnoticed last week. The athletes were required to name the shoe brand subsidizing them. This detail is required by authorities to avoid the unseemly sight of contracts broken at the last minute. Otherwise, officials fear, athletes might hold auctions to attract higher bidders, or compete in a preliminary heat with one brand, then switch to a more lucrative product for the prime-time final.

In the high-stakes world of "amateur" sports, such problems seem almost petty these days. The shoe-company reps who wielded awesome power only a few Olympiads ago are mere mom-and-pop operations compared to the corporate giants and meet promoters who have made millionaires out of some track stars. But shoe labels remain perhaps the most visible emblems of the wave of change. Every time one flashes across the screen in a subliminal commercial, it seems to stride a fine line between progress and corruption.

As America's corporations have weighed in with millions of dollars in subsidies, the general tendency has been to join in the cheerleading. In sheer jingoistic terms, it was deemed wonderful that our young people could at last be as well funded as their foes from the Eastern bloc. More thoughtful observers were delighted that at last the exploited athlete was reaping some of the riches that were once hoarded by meet directors or manufacturers. But some troubling contradictions linger.

[3]Reprint of an article by contributing editor Pete Axthelm and staff reporters. *Newsweek.* 104:68–9. Jl. 30, '84. Copyright © 1984 by Newsweek, Inc. All rights reserved. Reprinted by permission.

While Carl Lewis flaunts his collections of antiques and crystal, for example, athletes at lesser levels or in less glamorous sports still struggle to make ends meet. Edwin Moses soars over his hurdles with the name of his $100,000-a-year apparel sponsor emblazoned across his tank top, but Gerry Kiernan was disqualified after winning the Irish marathon trials while wearing a shoe-company logo on his T shirt—inadvertently and without remuneration. Because sports federations set their own peculiar rules, fans are left to puzzle over the discrepancies: pro-hockey players can skate into the Games as long as they haven't made the National Hockey league level, but pro-football players who have never been paid in track and field cannot run or jump for amateur medals.

In ruling against one such hurdler–football player, Renaldo Nehemiah, U.S. District Judge Clarkson Fisher cited "the pervasive hypocrisy of the so-called rules governing the amateur standing of participating athletes." But, he concluded, "if the plaintiff desires to play in Fantasyland, he must abide by the] rules."

Actually, hypocrisy and fantasy have always been entwined in the Olympic rings. Classicist David C. Young recently wrote a book aptly titled "The Olympic Myth of Greek Amateur Athletics." Young reports that some winners of the ancient Games took home fortunes. When Baron Pierre de Coubertin created the modern Games in 1896, Young says, he perpetrated "a kind of historical hoax." Coubertin's successors, most noisily the late Olympic czar Avery Brundage, were delighted to perpetuate the fraud; if a sprinter had to survive on handouts or a long jumper had to sell a medal to eat, banquet service was seldom interrupted in the International Olympic Committee chateau in Lausanne, Switzerland.

Soviet-bloc sports committees began taking advantage of such folly back in 1952, subsidizing their athletes to train full time, while Western athletes made do with meager under-the-table bribes. Then, in 1980, a new IOC president, Juan Antonio Samaranch of Spain, began to tinker with the rules and even things up. One of the few reformers ever to answer to His Excellency, Samaranch adopted a strategy roughly akin to states' rights: he decreed that the international federations for each sport could set their own rules.

The pro-hockey players at Sarajevo were in the vanguard of the new movement. But the International Amateur Athletic Federation, the ruling body for track and field, was also quick to open loopholes. As long as athletes were paid through cosmetic trust funds or expense-account schemes, they could be paid. Americans in particular quickly found armies of sponsors offering cash for meet appearances or the brandishing of company symbols.

There is little doubt that the new system produces better athletes as well as more conspicuous consumers. Not only can the athletes train better in lavish facilities, but they can stay in action longer, unencumbered by the prospect of seeking a day job. Brooks Johnson of Stanford, the Olympic women's track and field coach, says, "Mature people now, beyond the teeny-bopper stage, can make a dignified living at what they do best—run, jump and throw."

Not all collegiate observers are as sanguine. Because the National Collegiate Athletic Association hasn't sanctioned the IAAF-approved "trust funds," stars have an incentive to leave school and get rich quick. And the desire to keep a prized runner in school is one more inducement for desperate coaches to cheat.

The system also raises issues of priorities and fairness. For a year, U.S. soccer coach Manfred Schellscheidt developed an exuberant, hard-working "national team" of young amateurs. Then he was dumped in favor of Alkis Panagoulias, who kicked all but four of the amateurs off the squad and added 13 pros. Certainly the moonlighting pros will have a better medal chance. The crushed amateurs are left to wonder just what the rule makers—or American fans—really want from the Games. Shot-putter Brian Oldfield, 39, understands the left-out feeling, too. While the younger generation peddles its Olympic wares, Oldfield has been barred because he competed years ago in a short-lived, pro-track circuit, picking up a paltry $23,000.

One ready solution to such inequities is voiced by USOC president William Simon: "If we can't have honest amateurism, the Games should be open." The problem is that open participation would ruin the spirit and the entertainment value of some sports. Does anyone really want to see Larry Holmes savage the appealing young boxers that TV audiences have come to love? Or John

McEnroe give new meaning to the phrase "demonstration sport" as the Games apply it to tennis?

But perhaps such sacrifices are a price that must be paid. The Olympic movement has made welcome strides since the days when unbending old men held the sanctity of the amateur Games above athletes' welfare, human rights, even decent mourning for the Israelis who were slain in Munich. It is probably unfair to expect the forces of change to apply the brakes at precisely the right finish line. Buffeted by reality and politics, the Games may be cursed with confusion and hypocrisy as long as they exist. At least the new system makes their existence worth considering. Perhaps that will be one modest achievement to mark the 1984 Games in their imperfect world: this may be one time the Olympians almost got it right.

OVERHAUL THE OLYMPICS[4]

The Olympics need overhaul from top to bottom. Any attempt to do so will run into massive obstacles in the form of entrenched interests (on the part of officials, not competitors) and practical problems. A structure that is in place is hard to modify, even when it loses efficiency. Here are the trouble spots, along with good solutions, regardless of their attainability:

The problem: It has become prohibitively expensive to build new and complete Olympic facilities every four years in a different country, despite the hoped-for tourism benefits. The cost of the 1976 Games in Montreal is referred to as "scandalous" to this day, and there were so few bidders for the 1984 Games that Los Angeles got the nod after promising "austerity" and a minimum of government financing.

The solution: A permanent site in Greece is one obvious answer. It can be a single place, used for a single simultaneous multi-

[4]Excerpted from *Sports Illusion, Sports Reality* by Leonard Koppett, editor emeritus of the *Peninsula Times Tribune*, Palo Alto, California. Houghton Mifflin, 1981. Copyright © 1981 by Leonard Koppett. Reprinted by permission of Houghton Mifflin Company.

sport festival, like the Olympics we are used to. This would eliminate the cost of building afresh every four years and have the advantage of familiarity and continuity. But it would not alleviate the horrible logistical problems that go with gigantism.

The site can be several places, each tailored to a certain set of compatible sports, which can be used either simultaneously or at different times during the Olympic year. (We have this separation already, of necessity, for the Winter and Summer Games.) Or it can be a single place, but with the competition arranged sequentially rather than simultaneously.

Greece is an appropriate location, for historical and sentimental reasons. But there can be no guarantee that Greece, or any other country, won't be in an adversary relationship to many other countries, at some future time. In fact, it is as close to certain as anything can be that at least one country will find some other country objectionable every Olympiad.

No site on the national soil of any country can be divorced from that country's policies and laws at the time. It would be irresponsible and inconceivable for any government *not* to control events in its own territory. So for practical purposes the chosen single site, in Greece or whatever, should be ceded to some international entity, for whatever compensation may be agreed to, in order to create a living expression of the Olympic ideal that the Games are a holy truce from other conflicts.

Switzerland, it seems to me, has the experience with tourism to provide such a site if it is not internationalized, as well as a suitable climate for summer and winter competitions. Certainly the Winter Games could have a permanent home there. Some place along the Riviera, where France and Italy meet (and Monaco is located), might also work well, as might one of those spots around Switzerland's periphery that touches France, Italy, West Germany or Austria.

The legal and fiscal details of establishing such an international enclave should not be staggering, once there is a willingness to put the plan into effect.

The problem: If excessive nationalistic fervor has become a political liability, which it was in 1980, how can teams that do not exist except to represent countries in the Games be reconciled with

Olympic "brotherhood-of-man" idealism? In the original conception of the modern Olympics there was no room for team games, and even the notion of combining a number of individual results to form a team score (as with a track team) was rejected. The team idea, in both senses, gradually grew as the result of pressure from officials and followers of team sports who wanted a piece of the prestigious Olympic pie.

That, incidentally, is why no great effort has ever been mounted to push football and baseball into the Olympics. Their own successful commercial patterns were operating well enough to obviate the need for such recognition. Basketball and hockey, on the other hand, entered the Olympic stream when they were still trying to establish full commercial viability.

Unlike athletes in individual sports, team members represent *only* a national interest because the teams do not exist as entities before or after the Olympiad. It's hard to see how a team wearing a national uniform, composed of players brought together as all-stars exclusively on the grounds of citizenship for this one occasion, can help but inflame nationalism. The story of the 1980 U.S. hockey team is all the evidence anyone needs on this point.

The solution: Team sports should be separate, physically and theoretically, from individual sports. Whether or not we attach the word "Olympic" to what is actually perceived as a world championship is less important than making clear to all the distinction between team games and personal exploits.

If held at a different time and place from the individual events, Olympic team championships might even retain their nationalistic character without too much harm. In fact, world championships involving national teams are marvelous sports promotion. But if team sports are not totally separated from the other events, their national identities must be wiped out.

There is no reason why the basketball team must be *the* United States team. Let it be some existing team from within the United States (professional, if open competition comes about) and don't limit it to one team per country. Let the preliminary qualification process produce 16 or 35 teams regardless of their national origin. Many countries would have only one team to enter, but many might have more than one.

The essential requirement would be that the team's identity and basic composition has to be established for, say, at least two years prior to the Olympics. A preferable minimum in my opinion would be five years.

The problem: It doesn't constitute insult, provincialism or arrogant value judgment to insist that activities such as archery, shooting and yachting have different characteristics than track, basketball or swimming—in number of practitioners worldwide, amount of commercial attention and competitive format. To say they don't fit well under a single umbrella is to state the obvious. A jazz group, a marching band and a grand opera all have notable and distinct virtues and devotees. But we do not try to arrange major entertainment festivals that involve all three at once, under the same format.

The solution: The only answer to gigantism is diffusion. It is unrealistic to believe that all those who enjoy the benefits of the Olympic label will give it up, or that those who haven't had it yet will stop pursuing it. But there is no need to try to do everything at once.

The problem is essentially one of scheduling. What we need is an Olympic Year, not simply Summer and Winter Games. If, in each year divisible by four, we had a series of Olympic segments—one each month, or almost that—involving four or five appropriately related events, all sorts of difficulties would disappear. Logistics would be easier. Each sport would get a better piece of the worldwide stage while on it. And every group could pinpoint its preparations better, without coming into conflict with the needs of too many other groups (at the U.S. Olympic Training Centers, for instance).

The newly built central-site facilities would not have to be as large as those now required (since no brief maximum-occupancy period would occur) and would function for the full year, which is more efficient for all concerned. Skiing in January, skating and hockey in February, team sports in June, water sports in July, track and field in August, gymnastics in October—some such pattern would work like a charm.

The problem: Administrative problems boil down to problems of jurisdiction. As long as competitors (and officials) are classified according to citizenship, the problem of nationalism and its attendant political conflict cannot be dealt with.

But classifying entries according to citizenship is silly from the start. It's entirely possible that the four best sprinters in the world, all record breakers, will turn out to be United States citizens—or Jamaicans, or Nigerians, or Russians, or whatever. One of these would have to be left out, under present rules, while many lesser athletes would be included.

Furthermore, in today's world, people move from country to country—especially African and other non-American athletes recruited by American colleges. Citizenship hassles arise again and again, in all sorts of international competition, and many outstanding athletes have been victimized in the process. Why should the question of citizenship matter?

The International Olympic Committee could use a less nationalistic method for administering the Olympics. The solution is to do things a different way—but the problem is the IOC doesn't want to.

Most of the problems with the Olympics stem from the nature of this self-electing and self-perpetuating body that insists it has no obligations to any government or other group. It has a stranglehold on the world's national Olympic committees and international sports federations because of its power to bar anyone from the Olympics.

The IOC is a singularly undemocratic, archaic and secret body, unsuited in theory and in practice to the world of the 1980s. Some sort of reorganization, to make it more responsive to the will of competitors and of the governments who ultimately finance most Olympic activity, is inevitable.

The solution: In each of the last three Olympics, at least some of the greatest athletes in the world did not compete because their governments were for some reason engaging in a boycott. If a competitor is certified as "representing" Great Britain and the British government tells him not to go to Moscow, but the athlete (exercising his civil rights) does go, he has officially taken a position against his own government.

But if the athlete were certified as an individual, with no official mention of his nation or origin (as distinct from publicity mention, which is another matter), he would be taking a personal rather than a national stance. I don't suggest that this would help athletes from authoritarian states defy their governments, but it would certainly ease the situation in many countries.

So the proposal is to set up certification, and qualifying trials, by *region*, not by national boundaries. Have all applications go directly through international special-purpose committees, treating each applicant as an individual. It would then be the contestant's problem to get visas, satisfy the authorities at home, establish the proper public image and arrange his or her own financing.

Are these proposals practical and attainable within, let's say, ten years? I think so. If the United States and other like-minded countries insist hard enough, the rest have no choice but to go along.

BIBLIOGRAPHY

BOOKS AND PAMPHLETS

Anderson, Dave, ed. The Red Smith reader. Random House. '83.

Angell, Roger. Five seasons. Warner Books. '83.

Archer, Robert and Bouillon, Antoine. The South African game: sport and racism. Zed Press. '82.

Blanchard, Kendall and Cheska, Alyce. The anthropology of sport: an introduction. Bergin and Garvey. '84.

Cantu, Robert C. and Gillespie, W. Jay. Sports medicine, sports science: bridging the gap. Heath. '82.

Cashmore, Ernest. Black sportsmen. Routledge and Kegan. '82.

Coakley, Jay J. Sport in society: issues and controversies. Mosby. '82.

Considine, Tim. The language of sport. Facts on File. '83.

Darden, Ellington. The athlete's guide to sports medicine. Contemporary Books. '81.

Dyer, K. F. Catching up with the men: women in sport. State Mutual Books. '82.

Goldman, Bob and others. Death in the locker room: steroids and sports. Icarus. '84.

Goldstein, J. H., ed. Sports violence. Springer-Verlag. '83.

Halberstam, David. The amateurs: the story of four young men and their quest for an Olympic gold medal. William Morrow. '85.

Halberstam, David. The breaks of the game. Ballantine. '83.

Hargreaves, Jennifer, ed. Sport, culture, and ideology. Routledge and Kegan. '83.

Hazan, Baruch A. Olympic sports and propaganda games: Moscow 1980. Transaction Books. '82.

Hoberman, John M. Sport and political ideology. University of Texas Press. '84.

Lapchick, Richard. Broken promises: racism in American sports. St. Martin's. '84.

Lapchick, Richard E. The politics of race and international sport: the case of South Africa. Greenwood. '75.

Lipsky, Richard. How we play the game: why sports dominate American life. Beacon Press. '81.

Mandell, Richard D. Sport: a cultural history. Columbia Univ. Press. '84.

McGuane, Thomas. An outside chance: essays on sport. Farrar, Straus & Giroux. '80.

McMaster, James H. The ABCs of sports medicine. Krieger. '82.

Nixon, Howard L., II. Sport and the American dream. Leisure Press. '83.

Noverr, Douglas A. and Ziewacz, Lawrence. The games they played: sports in American history. Nelson-Hall. '83.

Patton, Phil. Razzle-dazzle: the curious marriage of television and professional football. Dial. '84.

Postow, Betsy C., ed. Women, philosophy and sport: a collection of new essays. Scarecrow. '83.

Powers, Ron. Supertube: the rise of television sports. Coward-McCann. '84.

Rader, Benjamin. American sports from the age of folk games to the age of spectators. Prentice-Hall. '83.

Rader, Benjamin. In it's own image: how television has transformed sports. Macmillan. '84.

Ryan, Frank. Sports and psychology. Prentice-Hall. '82.

Simon, Robert L. Sports and social values. Prentice-Hall. '85.

Snyder, Eldon E. and Spreitzer, Elmer A. Social aspects of sport. Prentice-Hall. '83.

Theberger, Nancy and Donnelly, Peter, eds. Sport and the sociological imagination. Texas Christian University Press. '84.

Thomas, Carolyn E. Sport in a philosophic context. Lea & Febiger. '83.

Welch, Paula and Lerch, Harold A. History of American physical education and sport. C. C. Thomas. '81.

PERIODICALS

Black Enterprise. 13:18. My. '83. Debate grows over Rule 48. R. McNatt.

Editorial Research Reports. v 1, no 4:67–84. Ja. 27, '84. Advances in athletic training. Marc Leepson.

Editorial Research Reports. v 2, no 9:655–672. S. 7, '84. New era in TV sports. Marc Leepson.

Humanist. 43:25+. Jl./Ag. '83. A humanistic approach to sports. Irving Simon.

Maclean's. 95:44. F. 1, '82. The limitless pay for play. Trent Frayne.

Maclean's. 96:72. S. 26, '83. When heroes become monsters. A. Fotheringham.

Ms. 11:92+. My. '83. When winning takes all. J. Levin.

Nation's Business. 70:14. N. '82. Of greenbacks and quarterbacks. James J. Kirkpatrick.

New Statesman. 108:8+. Ag. 10, '84. All-American dream. Eamon Dunphy.

New York Times. sec. 5, p 2. Jl. 4, '82. Keep the pros out of colleges. Bill L. Atchley.

New York Times. sec 5, p 3. Jl. 4, '82. The real problem: using drugs to win. Fred Dwyer.

New York Times. p 9+. O. 30, '82. The television dollars foster new perceptions. Neil Amdur.

New York Times. p D25. Ja. 18, '83. College "factories" and their output. Ira Berkow.

New York Times. p B11. Mr. 16, '83. A nation of sports fans. George Vecsey.

New York Times. sec 5, p 2. S. 4, '83. Drug testing cannot insure fair play. Harold Connolly.

New York Times. sec 5, p 2. S. 4, '83. Tests vindicate female athletes. Pat Connolly.

New York Times. sec 5, p 2. My. 26, '85. Medical problems of random drug tests. Dan Begel.

New York Times. p A10. My. 31, '85. British soccer fans: why so warlike? Jo Thomas.

New York Times. sec 5, p 2. Je. 2, '85. Why soccer serves as a vehicle for fan violence. Clive Toye.

New Yorker. 60:66+. S. 3, '84. If they don't win it's a shame. E. J. Kahn Jr.

Newsweek. 96:51. Ag. 11, '80. Cheating as an Olympic event. Pete Axthelm.

Newsweek. 101:64. Ja. 17, '83. Raising the grade for athletes. D. A. Williams.

Newsweek. 104:32-3. Ag. 13, '84. Red, white and blue TV. Harry F. Waters.

Newsweek. 104:15. Ag. 20, '84. Surprises of the spirit. Pete Axthelm.

Newsweek. 105:88. F. 4, '85. Exploring the racer's edge. George F. Will.

Penthouse. 15:144+. Ja. 1, '84. Advise & dissent: sports and drugs. Kareem Abdul-Jabbar.

Progressive. 48:50. My. '84. Going for the gold. Eugene J. McCarthy.

Psychology Today. 17:68. N. '83. A dangerous edge. J. C. Horn.

Psychology Today. 18:26. Jl. '84. The uses of anger: winning athletes turn rage into motivation and concentration. Edwin Kiester Jr.

Psychology Today. 18:28-32. Jl. '84. Beating slumps at their own game. Bruce C. Ogilvie and Maynard A. Howe.

Psychology Today. 18:36-39. Jl. '84. Courting the gods of sport. Judith Zimmer.

Psychology Today. 18:40. Jl. '84. Games athletes play. C. R. Creekmore.

Reader's Digest. 123:19-22. N. '83. The Olympics: unfair to women. Walter S. Ross.

Saturday Evening Post. 255:62-3. Jl./Ag. '83. Getting the Olympics back on track. J. Delmont.

Science News. 126:72. Ag. 4, '84. When is a drug a drug? J. Greenberg.

Skiing. 36:30-1. F. '84. Drug testing and the Games. R. E. Leach.

Sport. 72:10. F. '81. The violence act comes up short. Alan Page.

Sports Illustrated. 58:44-67. Ap. 11, '83. Too many punches, too little concern. Robert H. Boyle and Wilmer Ames.

Sports Illustrated. 59:15. Jl. 11, '83. Back to the Dark Ages. Jerry Kirshenbaum.

Sports Illustrated. 59:18–23. S. 5, '83. Caracas: a scandal and a warning. C. Neff.

Sports Illustrated. 60:36+. My. 28, '84. Taking steps to solve the drug dilemma. Jim Kaplan.

Time. 123:28–9. My. 21, '84. The agony of default. Tom Callahan and others.

Time. 123:61–2. Je. 25, '84. The toughest test for athletes. P. Stoler.

Time. 124:73. Ag. 20, '84. Out of the tunnel into history. Jane O'Reilly.

Time. 124:87. O. 29, '84. Take me out to the brawl game: violence at major sporting events seems to be on the rise. John Leo.

U. S. News & World Report. p 75–6. Ja. 24, '83. Classroom crackdown on college athletics. Alvin P. Sanoff.

U. S. News & World Report. 94:80. Mr. 28, '83. Megabucks for athletes. M. Stone.

U. S. News & World Report. 94:123–4. My. 9, '83. '84 summer Olympics, capitalist style. G. Bronson.

USA Today. 112:10–1. F. '84. Steroids: great risks to young athletes.

Vital Speeches of the Day. 49:504–7. Je. 1, '83. Academics and athletics; address Mr. 21, '83. Barbara S. Uehling.

Vogue. 174:219+. Jl. '84. Politics of sports. Janice Kaplan.

Vogue. 174:290. N. '84. The year of getting tough. Jane O'Reilly.

Wall Street Journal. p 26. Ja. 27, '83. Drug dealing and gambling in the NFL. Frederick Klein.

Washington Post. p C7. N. 21, '82. Barbaric pleasures. George F. Will.

Washington Post. p A23. My. 17, '84. Moral gymnastics. William F. Buckley Jr.

Women's Sports and Fitness. 6:32+. Jl. '84. 3,000 years in the making: the story of women at the summer Olympics. Michael Levy.

Women's Sports and Fitness. 6:47+. Ag. '84. Judgment day. Lee Green and Lesley Allen.

Womensports. 2:25+. S. '80. The right stuff. Linda Johnson.

World Press Review. 31:61. Mr. '84. Drugs and the Olympics. Ian Anderson.

World Press Review. 31:39+. Jl. '84. The politics of sport. James Christie.